Praise for Start

An outstanding book abou   , ...ng stories
to show what succeeds, wha. ....n t and why; a must-read for the
70 per cent of young people who want to be self-employed. ROGER
ALEXANDER, NON-EXECUTIVE CHAIRMAN, WALKER BOOKS, AND FORMER
CHAIRMAN, LEWIS SILKIN

A stimulating read about finding confidence and enjoying the
creative freedom of start-ups, pivots and pop-ups in realizing the
business you've always dreamed of living. ANNE BODDINGTON,
PROFESSOR OF DESIGN INNOVATION, PRO VICE-CHANCELLOR FOR
CULTURE AND PUBLIC ENGAGEMENT, AND DEAN, KINGSTON SCHOOL OF
ART, KINGSTON UNIVERSITY

If you've got that burning urge to run your own business and
follow an idea, this book will point you in the right direction. It
cannot tell you what to do, but it can help you understand your
own path and avoid the pitfalls of others. IAN PARKER, CHIEF
EXECUTIVE OFFICER, EQUITY RED STAR – THE INSURANCE COMPANY

A book crammed full of practical entrepreneurial wisdom. Helpful
pearls for anyone running a business or thinking of starting one.
KATE SHAND, CEO, ENJOY EDUCATION – LONDON'S AWARD-WINNING PRIVATE
TUITION AND HOME SCHOOLING COMPANY

'Do you want to make a difference? Do you want to feel
wonderful?' With words like these, Richard Hall and Rachel Bell
have created that rarest of business books, one that is informative,
engaging and inspiring. *Start-ups, Pivots and Pop-ups* is full of

helpful advice and wonderful encouragement for the journey to come. Whether you are thinking of creating your own business, looking to reinvent your current company or are just eager to learn more about this exciting topic, this is the book for you. MATTHEW MCCREIGHT, SENIOR PARTNER, SCHAFFER CONSULTING, STAMFORD, CONNECTICUT

A gift to anyone thinking about starting a business, this book is crammed full of brilliant advice from insightful folk who have been there, seen it and done it. Read *Start-ups, Pivots and Pop-ups* and be inspired to get on and make your business dreams a reality. PAM SCOBBIE, FOUNDER AND EXECUTIVE CREATIVE DIRECTOR, WIRE – 2019 MARKETING AGENCY OF THE YEAR

In a world exploding with possibilities, where the entrepreneurial spirit is the strongest it's ever been, this is the one book that helps frame the highs and the lows, and gives the truest insight and guidance from those who have tried and tried again to fight their way to success. ANGELA FARRUGIA, FOUNDER, TLC (THE LICENSING COMPANY)

We live with constant innovation in the film business. Our lives are full of risk, so I love the way Richard Hall and Rachel Bell write about the excitement of risking doing your own thing and creating something new. The world is changing. This book shows how to surf those changes. IAN GEORGE, MANAGING DIRECTOR, SONY PICTURES ENTERTAINMENT

A brilliant and insightful look behind the growth of some super-inspiring businesses, and an honest review of the mistakes their founders have made along the way. As a business owner, you need this book. MISHA DHANAK, FOUNDER, THE ROMANS – THE PR COMPANY

Richard Hall has mentored me for 20 years, constantly questioning my thinking and ambition, turning my corporate theory upside down, and he is brilliant, refreshing, energetic and insightful at it. Until June 2019, I was helping to sell as much cereal as possible as part of the FMCG world; now, my business goal is to build profitable eco-businesses from waste plastic. Richard and Rachel's book will be my bible. RUPERT MAITLAND-TITTERTON, EX-EUROPEAN COMMUNICATIONS DIRECTOR, KELLOGG'S; NOW EMBARKING ON A BRAVE NEW CAREER

Finally – a book that tells the truth about starting and running your own business, as told by real people who have done it. Inspiring, sobering, revealing, and an absolute must-read for all entrepreneurs at whatever stage of the journey they are on. GARY BOOKER, CHIEF MARKETING, INNOVATION AND STRATEGY OFFICER, RENTOKIL INITIAL

Step aside MBA homeboys – the real entrepreneurs have arrived. A straight-up, myth-busting account of the realities of modern start-ups, this book is indispensable for anyone thinking about starting their own business. DAVE FLETCHER, FOUNDER AND CEO, WHITE OCTOBER – THE DIGITAL PRODUCT CONSULTANCY

Rachel Bell has been my number one business inspiration – she helped me believe I could go out on my own and shine, and I did. For anyone toying with the idea of starting a business, do yourself a favour and read this book. RONKE OKE, FOUNDER, EMI & BEN

The world I am seeing is changing fast... and faster! With this come unique demands and customer needs. And more importantly, opportunities to meet unmet needs. Start-ups and new ventures meet these challenges quicker and better than traditional legacy corporates. *Start-ups, Pivots and Pop-ups* therefore could not come at a better time; it is full of entertaining stories, all bringing to life the pragmatic recipe for how to be a successful entrepreneur, a fulfilled individual. Full of optimism and inspiration, it is a must-read. ALEX PORACCHIA, PARTNER, DELOITTE FINANCIAL SERVICES AND INSURANCE

Start-ups, Pivots and Pop-ups

How to succeed by creating your own business

Richard Hall and Rachel Bell

KoganPage

Publisher's note

Every possible effort has been made to ensure that the information contained in this book is accurate at the time of going to press, and the publishers and authors cannot accept responsibility for any errors or omissions, however caused. No responsibility for loss or damage occasioned to any person acting, or refraining from action, as a result of the material in this publication can be accepted by the editor, the publisher or the authors.

First published in Great Britain and the United States in 2020 by Kogan Page Limited

2nd Floor, 45 Gee Street	122 W 27th St, 10th Floor	4737/23 Ansari Road
London	New York, NY 10001	Daryaganj
EC1V 3RS	USA	New Delhi 110002
United Kingdom		India

www.koganpage.com

© Richard Hall and Rachel Bell, 2020

The right of Richard Hall and Rachel Bell to be identified as the authors of this work has been asserted by them in accordance with the Copyright, Designs and Patents Act 1988.

ISBNs

Hardback	978 1 78966 032 6
Paperback	978 0 7494 9746 0
eBook	978 0 7494 9745 3

British Library Cataloguing-in-Publication Data

A CIP record for this book is available from the British Library.

Library of Congress Cataloging-in-Publication Data

Library of Congress Cataloging-in-Publication Data is available for this book.
Control Number: 2019036564.

Typeset by Integra Software Services, Pondicherry
Print production managed by Jellyfish
Printed and bound by CPI Group (UK) Ltd, Croydon CR0 4YY

Most people find their biggest disappointment in life is their caution – the things they didn't do, rather than those they did. We encourage you all to be bold, to dream, to explore your talent and to find your true potential as an independent spirit.

Contents

About the authors

Richard Hall

After Balliol College, Oxford, Richard's early career was in learning and practising marketing with blue chip FMCG companies like Reckitt's and RHM Foods. A lengthy spell in advertising followed, with leading roles in French Gold and Abbott, FCO and Havas. In the latter part of his career Richard was asked to act as non-executive chairman in several marketing services companies and two charities, was a co-founder of a consultancy start-up and, finally, has written a raft of business books published in over 20 countries. He has also created a mentoring business which flourishes. Retirement? As Confucius said, 'Choose work that you love and you won't have to work another day'. Richard has and he doesn't. The work he does is much too much fun.

Rachel Bell

At an early age Rachel learnt the art of customer service in the hospitality industry and one other big lesson – the harder you work and the more you get done, the faster you get on. Rachel has started six multi-award-winning comms businesses – the most notable being PR agency Shine. Her philosophy of promoting and developing talent has won her industry recognition including #1 *Sunday Times* Best Small Company to Work For. She is a serial NED and chairs CIS, her late father's engineering business. She was nominated best leader of a small business in 2012 by the *Sunday Times*. She is currently also working with the London Business School, inspiring MBA students in entrepreneurship.

Prologue

Review of the potential for starting a new business and the enterprise *zeitgeist*

We live in exciting times. There has never been so much uncertainty. But equally there have never been so many opportunities. What we are witnessing is an explosive growth in the desire for independence. This makes things tough for the big corporations. Stephanie Atkinson, HR Director of Kellogg's European Functions, described a graduate intern who was very talented and doing well. After a year, to everyone's disappointment, she resigned. 'Why?' they asked, imploring her to stay. She said she loved the company, its culture and all the people she worked with; however, she'd learnt a lot but needed to move on and learn more and different things.

The word career means less and is decreasingly relevant to many. This will make it tough to attract and keep the best talent. More and more people (and not just the young) are questioning the big company where 'right sizing' is the polite word for describing the frequent round of redundancies and where the decision-making processes are turgidly slow. Will Arnold-Baker, ex Managing Director of Publicis UK, who's started his own advertising agency together with two colleagues, put it simply:

> As we won yet another account (at Publicis) I asked myself why I was doing it for them and not for us?

So they set up the bravely named 'Come the Glorious Day' advertising agency in 2017. And they're having fun, winning business, hiring people, making money, but are rather short of sleep.

The old world is being disrupted. It's a revolution not a lateral swing of the pendulum. This is a world where Yvon Chouinard's company 'Patagonia', the running of which he so brilliantly describes in his book *Let My People Go Surfing*, becomes a role model rather than a crazy fantasy. We are living in a world where all the smart money is on catching the wind in our sails. What are we waiting for?

Explore. Dream. Discover.

Who and where we are and why we wrote this book

Rachel Bell is a well-known figure in the PR industry and has been the author of several successful agency start-ups. She is now Chair of the Academy (the PR company) and a serial NED. She is also a visitor in entrepreneurship at The London Business School.

Richard Hall is an author of several business books that have been published in over 20 countries. Previously he had a career in marketing, advertising and consultancy. He coaches executives in how to win in an increasingly competitive world.

Rachel spends most of her working life in London, but her main home is in Somerset. Nearby Bristol and Bath are becoming increasingly noted for their entrepreneurial achievements, and SETsquared, the Bristol incubator, has won global applause as the best incubator partnership in the world.

In 2011 HSBC published a report on the 'Future of Business in Britain'. Brighton was nominated as one of five supercities. In 2012 Bristol joined Brighton as one of HSBC's supercities.

Richard lives in Brighton, the cryptic accolade to which in the HSBC report, read 'the capital of the UK's rebellious, alternative economy'. Since that report, Brighton has lived up to its billing, enjoying vigorous growth and extensive infrastructure investment. Turnover in tech is rising fast (currently at over £600 million) and there were over 200 start-ups in 2017. Key sectors have been gaming and virtual reality. Here's the sort of press the city gets:

> Brighton is one of the most diverse, cosmopolitan, green, liberal and exciting cities in the UK…leading the way with a raft of new openings, pop-ups…demonstrating the appetite for independent operators and home grown talent. (Dowd, 2019)

The emphasis on Brighton and Bristol in *Start-ups, Pivots and Pop-ups* is owing to our local knowledge but equally because both cities are representative of what Britain, outside London, could become in the future. Enterprising, innovative and, perhaps, a little 'rebellious' as well.

Why we needed to write this book

Independently of each other, we'd both been feeling the pulse of a disrupted workplace. We'd been seeing the desire that people had to run their own businesses. We talked about the impact of rewarding and motivating talented people and splitting off parts of a business to kick-start new businesses.

But we wanted to be more than spectators. We wanted to get amongst it and encourage more people to have the courage to be proactive, to find the energy required and seek the thrill of starting their own businesses. We also thought that there were too many Clever-Dick-How-To-Get-Rich entrepreneur books around. We wanted to explore 'the thinking and philosophy' not just the 'how to' of starting a business.

We wanted to explore the experimental phases of 'pop-ups' that are increasingly popular. Just go to Pop-Up-Brixton and you'll see what we mean. And finally, the essential but relatively new word in business, 'pivoting'. All too often this can be a fancy way of describing 'changing your mind'. But we think it means so much more. It's the strategic equivalent of tacking in sailing – going where the wind can do most for you.

We do not pretend that starting a new business is easy. It requires a vision, enormous energy, self-belief and great tactical execution. Too often bad or sloppy business practice wrecks a neat idea. We hope to create a cocktail of inspiration, pragmatic tips and tactics to help other start-ups to want to win and then actually do it.

We have interviewed around 100 start-up business people. And guess what? We have been so excited by them that we almost want to start a business all over again ourselves and 'sail away from safe harbour'. The people we've talked to have been so enthusiastic that it just seems so exciting.

But first we had this book to write...

What we want this book to do

Sell lots obviously.

But more to the point, we want it to be the definitive and inspiring guide to starting a business. This is a story about an adventure, a flight into the unknown like space travel. Here's what Giuseppe Cocconi and Philip Morrison said in their paper in 1959, 'Searching for interstellar communications':

> The probability of success is difficult to estimate; but if we never search the chance of success is zero.

The thrill of searching for success, of going on a lonely, intrepid mission and of discovering something new and wonderful can only be understood by someone with the experience of such a journey.

This book will help you get a taste for success and excitement. It will act as a flight manual but it's not prescriptive. It looks at the world of start-ups, pop-ups and pivots from a series of perspectives. It's not just about the UK. It's about the opportunities that the whole world offers.

In writing it we've met and talked to great talent and discovered many things, not least that there is no simple formula for success. Instead, there are a series of rocks and hazards that you need to avoid and beware of. Not least this, our first simple piece of advice.

Keep your wits about you. Never think you've got it made, that's the biggest mistake you could ever make. Here's what Andy Grove ex CEO and Chairman of Intel said:

> Success breeds complacency. Complacency breeds failure. Only the paranoid survive. (Sager, 2007)

Here's our second simple piece of advice. We've got to believe in ourselves.

Sometimes it's hard to retain the confidence that will help us win. Lord Denning, regarded by many as the greatest judge in the UK in the 20th century, told young barristers that people paid for certainty not for doubts.

Enthusiasm, energy and confidence are the winning qualities.

CHAPTER ONE

The ups and downs of starting a new business

A story about a successful start-up

Much of this book uses real-life examples of start-ups, starting, faltering, pivoting and, more often than not, succeeding. Here's the first story that contains everything. A long apprenticeship, a pivot, a jump into the void with a 'pop-up', success followed by a Black Swan[1] of a company destroyer, followed by an example of ingenuity, a start-up and then a long journey to solid success.

Monty's Bakehouse

Monty's Bakehouse creates and provides premium snacks and food for the travel industry, primarily airline companies. The business started in 2003 and is based in West Sussex. The story starts a lot earlier.

Dad shows the way

Matt Crane, the founder, talks fondly of his Dad who dabbled in business, invented stuff and had a journey of rags to riches to rags. Matt describes home being, one moment a mansion and then a cottage. It was, he said, great fun. Matt like so many successes in life did not shine at school where his talent wasn't spotted. The literal translation of the word 'educate' is to draw out. Two Es at A level showed no sign of drawing much out, yet he 'scraped' into university where he embraced the freedom in contrast to school and educated himself, joyfully getting a good 2.1 in Biology and Biochemistry.

He also showed early signs of entrepreneurial flair when he picked up some rusting tandem bikes from a scrap dealer for a song, refurbished them and fixed aluminium panels on them on which he painted the coat of arms of leading Cambridge University colleges. These customized bikes produced £800, a massive return on investment. His Dad approved of activities like this but gave him great advice:

> Don't do it my way – go and get jobs where you learn a lot and where you make your mistakes at someone else's expense.

Getting grounded before taking off

Matt spent 16 years learning some important stuff: three years in graphic design (all his structural and graphic design work is done in-house at Monty's Bakehouse); four years in sales promotion and marketing communication at Triangle; six years working as Stores Format Director at Safeway Supermarkets working on assignment from McKinsey; and three years as Marketing Director at TXU Europe – the Texas Energy Company.

Quite simply he had taken his father's advice. He was learning to design, innovate and to market. He was equipped and ready to swim with the sharks in a start-up. He considered the opportunities in the snacks and juices markets, researching both.

He started to work seriously on these two, inspired and being kept going by people around him who constantly told him he was uniquely driven.

'It all happened by accident'

That's what Matt said, but it's more interesting than mere happenstance. He loved rugby and he also loved sausage rolls and the whole idea of grab-and-go food. So, on the basis of 2+2=4, he set up a pop-up stall at Twickenham Stadium selling his own recipes of sausage rolls during the internationals. It went so well he eventually had six kiosks. Pop-up had become popping-up-all-over. 'Did it make money?' we asked. He laughed dryly, 'Nope. Great customer flow, great cash flow, high costs and measly margin'. Then things got worse. Legislation was introduced in the early 2000s for hygiene reasons that prevented the same person selling unwrapped food and taking the money for it. So, there'd be no more Twickenham sausage rolls unless he doubled his staff. But what happened (not really by accident) was Matt worked on researching how to find a solution to this 'challenge'. He discovered a newish, polyethylene material in which you could wrap snacks and cook them at temperatures up to 200 degrees Celsius. Problem solved. No hands touching the food.

Back to Twickenham in 2002 where Matt was giving a great show of producing delicious hot hygienic snacks, providing high class customer service but hardly making enough money to make it worthwhile. One day, in a lull in activity, Matt noticed a man staring at what he was doing. He walked across and asked Matt a few searching questions about the business and the packaging. Then he walked away and shook his head a few times like someone having an 'aha!' moment, before coming back and handing Matt his card. It said, 'Inflight Director Air Canada'. He asked Matt to call him when he had a moment.

How much?!

So, a few days later, Matt called. He was asked to come into an office near Heathrow and talk about his business to a few people. Matt had learnt a lot about pitching at the marketing company he'd worked for, so he prepared properly although he was still pretty uncertain what this was about. Those few people turned out to be a roomful of executives. Matt says that even he was impressed by his performance that day. He described how everyone seemed fascinated by the quality of the snacks and the polyethylene wrapping that seemed to solve the tricky problem of serving hot snacks at 35,000 feet, quickly and cleanly.

A few days later he got a call. After the niceties he was told Air Canada would like to place an order. He stopped breathing and heard a croaking voice (his own) ask how much for. At the other end of the line a calm voice said Air Canada would like to place an order for 13 pallets to be delivered fortnightly for the first 12 months.

That was a mountain of snacks, an edible Everest. And he hadn't got the gear in place to climb a hill yet, let alone a mountain.

We have lift off...

He and his wife sat down and worked out how much money they could raise quickly by remortgaging their house, delving into Matt's pension pot and borrowing from family and friends. He then worked out the logistics of production, packaging, delivery, of creating a new firm to manage this huge piece of business. He didn't sleep much for a few days. He and his wife constantly looked at each other in a mixture of terror and delight. This was it: the opportunity to have a real business created with a real, substantial flow of regular income from a blue chip client.

Like all well-trained business people, Matt could create great plans. He said that whilst you knew it wouldn't turn out quite the way you planned, at least you knew where the stress points were, what was missing and how you should monitor progress.

How a pop-up becomes a real start-up

Today Monty's Bakehouse has 50 direct employees; produces between 35 and 40 million meals a year – that's over 100,000 daily; and has clients like Air Canada (of course), BA, Cathay Pacific, SAS, Scandinavian, Qatar. Monty's Bakehouse products are also served in big event stadiums and in high-end bakery retailers. Matt decided to separate creative development and production. The capital investment in setting up industrial-scale kitchens was a reach too far, and besides there are some great producers out there. What he concentrated on was the way to reinvent sausage rolls and grab-and-go food with great looking, brilliantly packed snacks. The business depends on finding new recipes and winning respect for what they do. In 2016 they won the Mercury Award for best inflight snack with their Chinese BBQ Chicken Savoury Pastry. It sounds simple. Looking back on where they were 16 years ago, however, when it was exciting but full-on and absolutely terrifying, the journey has become an exhilarating rollercoaster ride.

Matt has these key observations, 'We have to keep our business, our food and the way we work *relevant* the whole time'.

We love that word 'relevant'. In a world where artificial intelligence and robotics are constant topics of conversation and where it's difficult as a customer to get to talk to a human being (especially in large institutions), it's unsurprising that so many people are worried about the relevance of their jobs. Between 1760 and 1820 in the Industrial Revolution the workers in Britain were going through similar moments of self-doubt. Matt is very clear about one thing, 'This is not an asset or a brand business, it's a people business'.

It started with a human being pitching his product and winning a big piece of business. Sixteen years later he still has the Air Canada business. Without great human interfaces, client management and a creative workplace, this might not be the case.

The entrepreneurial landscape

> Many entrepreneurs are reckless, impetuous and selfish and they
> crash through life leaving chaos in their wake.

This is what Guy Singh-Watson, the founder of Riverford Organic Food Service and Farms, said to Kirsty Young on BBC Radio
4's *Desert Island Discs*, on 6 July 2018. We tend to agree with
Guy. To many, an entrepreneur is characterized by a swaggering
rebelliousness, a very low boredom threshold, a gambling streak
and an obsession with money. We know entrepreneurs who have
towering rages and the attention span of minutes. They're rich
but unhappy. At the very centre of this book is an ongoing
conversation about work–life balance and happiness. Some are
convinced that anyone who works for themselves is bound to be
a workaholic. Then there are others, which include us and Simon
Sinek, who see it slightly differently, claiming it's only working
hard at something that you don't really care about that creates
imbalance and stress, whilst working hard at something you do
really care about still creates imbalance, but imbalance and
passion. Sinek thinks the passion compensates for the imbalance. Meanwhile, Kirstin Furber, former Head of People at
ClearScore and BBC Worldwide, says everyone in HR is currently
talking about something called 'One Life' where work and life
blur into one happy cocktail.

We want to distinguish between the cowboys whose interest
is in a quick 'exit' and the people who are trying to build their
own *sustainable* business. We detest the casual use of that word
'exit' by the way. If we hear someone using it as their primary
objective for being an entrepreneur, we steer well clear of them.
They're not creating a business; they're playing a game of business poker.

The real start-up engineers, in whom we're most interested,
are full of enterprise, ambition and hope. They are opportunity

creators. They are like us. They want to leave a legacy. They are not 'risk averse' like their counterparts in big companies. The old-fashioned flash entrepreneur is dying out and being usurped by hard-working, smart, collaborative, creative and independently minded pioneers who want to change the world (a little, not a lot – they aren't that unrealistic). They want to be proud of what they do because they prize being liked. In a way they are returning themselves to their very roots. Here's how Mohammad Yunus, the Bangladeshi entrepreneur, founder of the Grameen Bank and Nobel Peace Laureate, put it in a *Guardian* interview (Cosic, 2019), celebrating Yunus receiving the Concordia Leadership Award during their 2016 Summit:

> *The old-fashioned flash entrepreneur is dying out and being usurped by hard-working, smart, collaborative, creative and independently minded pioneers.*

> All human beings are entrepreneurs. When we were in the caves we were all self-employed…finding our food, feeding ourselves. That's where the human history began…as civilization came we suppressed it. We became labour because [they] stamped us, 'you are labour'. We forgot that we are entrepreneurs.

Yes. We are all innately entrepreneurs; let's understand what that could mean for those of us who dare to try to be innovators. But first of all, beware. In an article in *The Times* 'Dream of Being an Entrepreneur? Trust Me, They Dream of Being You', Sathnam Sanghera warns entrepreneur wannabes against expecting freedom (Sanghera, 2019). He recalls that it was the tyranny of accounting, managing people and navigating health and safety regulations that drove restaurateur Raymond Blanc to a minor stroke in his forties. Do not become an entrepreneur, Sanghera says, unless you are willing to work incredibly, crazily hard.

For our part, we think we are that hard. So, let's move on.

Who? Where? How? What?

Who are we talking about? The enterprise line-up

There are many types of start-up person and entrepreneur, and we list eight below. Most of these are well known, but we want to focus on three as we have most to learn from them.

I) YOUNG AND HUNGRY

These are bright, young people leaving school to fulfil a dream, or going to university to do 'Business Studies'. Some say going out to work in a start-up is much more interesting than the course work, which is, perhaps, unsurprising. Having said that, a lot of these types say the basic groundwork and debates around business topics have shaped the way they approach real work-life issues. One of our contributors, Chris Hannaway, stuck with it at Bath University to graduate in Business Administration, having set up a worthwhile business in his own year out. But he's now on his second start-up (an alcohol-free beer business). More of him later.

Of course, there's a practical issue. If you graduated after 2012 you don't start repaying your student loan until you earn over £25k pa, which you're unlikely to do soon if you're starting a new business.

II) IDEALISTS

Some of these are social entrepreneurs who want to change the world. Some are rebels. Some are romantics. However, a surprising number are confident individualists who are making a courageous lifestyle choice in striking out on their own (or in partnership). Money seems a prime motivator to far fewer people than we'd have expected.

III) SECOND-LIFE EXECUTIVES

Across the world, do not expect to survive long in corporate life when you are over 50, being well paid, in a senior position, but not going any further. In the last century in Japan, such people were given, what was nominated, 'a seat by the window' (a better place to be because, with brighter light, it was easier to read the newspaper) and were given the task of schmoozing customers whilst others worked.

Across the world, do not expect to survive long in corporate life when you are over 50, being well paid, in a senior position, but not going any further.

The middle-aged are vulnerable and rueing our opening words to this book as they grasp their redundancy package and plan the start-up that they should have done back in their thirties when they were young, idealistic and not cloned into being a corporate executive. These words ring in their ears, 'Most people find their biggest disappointment in life is their caution – the things they didn't do, rather than those they did'.

Relax. You can become human again and discover your real talents.

IV) OLDER AND BORED

Data shows increasing numbers of retirees are starting businesses and fulfilling dreams, hobbies or ambitions they'd never previously fulfilled. 'Magazine-Brighton' is a shop near Brighton's station that has been in existence for four years now. They sell a 400+ selection of independent magazines published internationally. It's an older man's dream fulfilled and it's succeeding.

For many, the thought of being a golf-playing retiree whose brain is in neutral and whose days are numbered is anathema. If starting a business is not high on the agenda, then mentoring or advising a start-up may be. *Forbes* magazine (Akalp, 2019) ran an article that concluded:

[a]ccording to a *Gallup study*, baby boomers are twice as likely to want to start a business in the next year than millennials. People over 50 represent one of the fastest-growing groups of entrepreneurs in the United States.

V) WOMEN (INCREASINGLY AND IMPORTANTLY)

Margaret Heffernan, in her 2008 book *Women on Top*, quotes some statistics about the United States where 40 per cent of all privately held companies are controlled by women, and women's companies are more likely to stay in business than men's. Her book is over 10 years old but still relevant. Increasingly, women are not so much breaking the glass ceiling as slipping out of that glass-ceilinged room to start their own business, on their own terms.

Unsurprisingly, that bellwether, the *Financial Times*, organized the 'FT Women at the Top' summit at the Landmark Hotel in 2018. But we suspect the *FT*, being a corporate, is still thinking corporately. The power of women in the entrepreneurial space is hot news right now. In our own interviews, the women have shone brightly in their professionalism, thoroughness and maturity. The difficulty they face is that men (in general) control the money in this world (bankers, VCs, funders) and these funders of business want fast results. According to Professor Elisabeth Kelan, Professor of Leadership and Organisation at Essex Business School, University of Essex, data shows that women's start-ups tend to grow more slowly than men's would do in the same situation. Yes…but pause and look back at that statistic from Heffernan: '40 per cent of all privately held US companies are controlled by women and women's companies are more likely to stay in business than men's'.

Do you want a flash in the pan or a sound, well-run, sustainable business? It's your choice, or rather it's the choice of funders who up to now have seemed rather to favour flash in the pans.

VI) SERIAL PROFESSIONALS

You see some of these on *Dragon's Den*. You'll see a lot of them doing MBAs. At any Soho House around the world, Home House and other trendy watering holes, you'll find people planning their next move. We are not antagonistic about their efforts and success. They are mostly men and they are driven to make fast money. But this book is addressed to a wider, more diverse audience than this MBA superclass.

VII) CHANCERS

These are the traders, the set-it-up-and-move-on characters. They have a big role in the black economy and the economy at large. They are the ones with incredibly short attention spans and a strong sense of opportunism. They have a nose for business, but they are not creators and business builders. They are not the future.

VIII) LOSERS

In conversation with Gordon Marsden, MP for Blackpool South, historian and expert on education and community affairs, he observed a problem in his constituency, namely the large number of people who, after being made redundant, set up businesses but without a plan, without having thought it through and with no experience of what people really want to buy and how to market to them. This has broader relevance too. It's a tragedy of ignorance amongst inexperienced people suddenly out of work and desperate to try something new. This is the flip side of our optimistic take on the enterprise economy. And it's a business opportunity for people to set up proper help and advice to start-ups – businesses like Merlie Calvert's company Farillio, the legal advice company for impoverished start-ups in the tech space in London. Fortunately, there are exceptions in Blackpool, like Montague's Beach Bar and Restaurant whose website and Trip Advisor reviews suggest this is a class act.

Focusing on those three key entrepreneurial cohorts

Millennials: why they matter so much

Simon Sinek's conversation about 'millennials' is one of the most viewed pieces on YouTube, being both funny and insightful. But that was 2016 and things are changing fast. Most young people are no longer snowflakes. We are seeing a tougher, kinder, smarter, less 'entitled', more collaborative generation coming through. But – and it's a big but – Princes Trust CEO, Martina Milburn, said in 2017, 'there's been a staggering deterioration in young people's confidence in themselves and in their future'.

But not many young people that we've talked to are like that. We wonder if the downbeat stories about knife crime and snowflakes has got in the way of an awkward truth for an older generation. That millennials are the very welcome future. Because we think that this is the clearest-thinking, kindest and most energetic young generation we've ever seen. Here are two examples to make our point.

Daisy Stapley-Bunten, who's the editor of *Start-Up Magazine*, is 24 and she's flying. She's smart, resourceful and mature in her thinking. She also has that quality of resilience Sinek denies these young people have.

Hugh Duffie in North London is running his own cold filtered coffee business and is living in a close knit community. 'I don't know anyone in a big company. All my friends are running their own businesses or are working in a start-up.'

Collaboration, idea-sharing and bartering have become the way they live. They are creators not takers. They are hard-working, idealistic and making their world on their terms.

Some like Harry Maitland in Liverpool are a special phenomenon. Harry is 18. He got a cluster of A*and As in GCSE and A levels. Clearly old-fashioned minds would have thought him Oxbridge material. But Harry is also a drummer in a Rock Band (Rats). They are aspiring towards possible success using a marketing formula so well thought through it would put most other start-ups to shame. Years ago, Nick D'Aloisio made £30 million from an AI development called *Summly* when he was 15. He was modest, smart and focused on what he should do. Harry's rather like him.

Don't expect many of these millennials to be great at envelope licking or be subservient employees. Don't expect what we used to call loyalty from them. Just watch in amazement at the new world that they're going to build.

Women: that glass ceiling. A glass myth. And a glass of champagne

Read Tom Peters' *Re-imagine!* (2003) for an impassioned prediction that the future lies with women. Now around 20 years later, not much has changed. Indeed, the World Economic Forum predicted in 2017 that it would take over 200 years for gender pay equality to be completely fulfilled (Treanor, 2019). For sure the gender pay gap and lack of top female jobs is still out of kilter with reality, with only 6 per cent of FTSE 100 CEOs being women, but things are changing (Chapman, 2019). But isn't it worth asking if that 6 per cent would be a bigger number if so many talented women hadn't concluded that climbing that greasy corporate pole wasn't for them?

Start-ups, Pivots and Pop-ups examines, amongst other things, the opportunities and challenges women face. It tells the story of glass ceilings, glass cliffs and anything else that describes how hard it's been for them to break through. But most of all, it tells the story of how women are writing their own narrative now and have increasingly become a driving force in the start-up world.

Women are writing their own narrative now and have increasingly become a driving force in the start-up world.

The stories we have are rich, vivid and varied. But above all, many of the new female entrepreneurs have learnt their stuff in big companies and are equipped with skills and experience.

Some, with children now at school, are itching to do something new, something they control, like their own business. Some are simply driven to create something better, something new and something that has lasting value.

We should raise a glass to them. They, particularly, and the millennials are changing the way we do things and the way we think about the business world.

Experienced ex-executives: Why experience is a magic sauce

All the data we have from the National Bureau of Economic Research in the United States says the more experienced you are the better the chance of success in starting a new business. The difference in failure rates between under 30-year-olds and over 30-year-olds is a significant 7 per cent. Despite their greater energy and lack of family ties, youth doesn't have all the advantages. Remember what Matt Crane's Dad said, 'Learn and make your mistakes at other people's expense'.

Too many of the degrees in entrepreneurship are gained by people who are bright but inexperienced in starting a business, except on paper. California-based Zach Rosner, on the other hand, although still in his early thirties, is embarked on a major start-up but has previously worked as HR Head in a Digitally Native Vertical Brand[2] start-up MeUndies – reinventing the underwear market for men and women – and before that at Everlane and Frog. He is not a start-up virgin. He knows and has circumvented some of the practical dangers and traps that await the young entrepreneur.

Have you got what it takes to succeed?

Are there too many entrepreneurs nowadays?

Certainly, there are too many people plunging into the icy sea before they've learnt to swim. To do a start-up properly needs a lot of time, advice, thinking, debate and some money too. There are people watching George Clooney (who's just made up to a billion dollars selling his Tequila brand, Casamigos), Elon Musk, Jack Ma (of Alibaba fame) and Sir James Dyson who think the descriptor 'entrepreneur' is a glamorous and cool handle in dinner party conversation:

'What do you do?'
'Me? I'm an entrepreneur.'
'Ooh. Like Richard Branson.'
'Yeah I guess so.'

In fact, the word originates from the French 19th century from *entreprendre*, which means 'to undertake'. More recently it has come to mean, 'A person who sets up a business or businesses, taking on financial risks in the hope of profit'.

There are too many so-called entrepreneurs around for sure. Beware those who preen themselves when they say that's what they are. Starting a business from scratch is one of the most challenging and difficult things people can do. Yes, it's thrilling, but it is hard. The careless use of the word entrepreneur is a pigeonhole like 'rock star' that's best avoided until you've really made it.

Spotting entrepreneurialism in the very young

We were interested to know if it is possible to detect early signs of enterprise. We heard, for instance, of an early sign of junior enterprise discovered by a father on holiday when he found his 7-year-old son was buying cheap sunglasses, selling them to people round a pool and then reinvesting his profits in more sunglasses.

Vicki Harrocks teaches performance arts at the school that was voted the most creative in 2018, Formby High School, Merseyside, and she reckons as early as year 6 she can spot the pupils who are potential entrepreneurs. They are, she says, those who are a little rebellious, questioning and disruptive, not because they're naughty but because they get ideas fast and want to talk about them. Most of all they are fearless presenters and performers. Drama, music and dance are essential to their development.

Mastering the ego: the art of reinvention

The biggest problem with being 'reduced' from a corporate Superman with all the executive trimmings to 'Rachel or Richard Who? And what's the name of your company?' can be hard to take when we're used to people being impressed by our saying, 'I'm a Director of the Global Enterprise Corporation'. This is something Tom discovered:

Tom was a success. He had a huge office, a PA, an executive assistant, a rather big salary, luxury car, membership of clubs, social and golf, his company sponsored test cricket, so he knew all the stars, he was a regular and fêted speaker at conferences, and he was a NED of several companies. He was, in short, a hero.

When he lost his job, the perks and his reputation, which was somewhat tarnished, he found himself feeling very lonely.

He was just another portfolio guy.

To succeed we have to reinvent ourselves and replace that Master of the Universe swagger with an energetic, enthusiastic and liberated persona.

This is all about moving from the C-suite to working on a laptop in Starbucks. There's either a sad, slightly humiliating story here or, instead, an opportunity for a refreshing change of focus. To succeed we have to reinvent ourselves and replace that Master of the Universe swagger with an energetic, enthusiastic and liberated persona. Think freedom not loss.

Why ambition matters

The world is full of solid businesses that grow slowly (investors hate these). Then, there are businesses that with investment and courage could achieve greater scale and achieve a fast exit (investors like these). Wall Street bursts a collective blood vessel when a company like Apple or Kellogg's misses a quarterly profit forecast. But Julian Richer, founder and CEO of Richer Sounds, shows in his 2019 book *The Ethical Capitalist* that it's possible to reconcile business and ethics to the benefit of customers, employees and suppliers. So long as we believe that only quarterly forecasts are what matter we shall create a rather lopsided world. Richer put his money where his mouth is when, in May 2019, he gave 60 per cent of his company shares to his employees in a £3.5 million windfall for them (Parry, 2019).

Zach Rosner, the co-founder of Zacom in California, said he liked the idea of building a sustainably cash-generative business. Others are happy merely to survive. Many are trapped between the siren calls of hungry funders and cautious management and are concerned to create a family of customers and employees. In Germany they call this latter group *Mittelstand*. The classic SME-type *Mittelstand* companies with turnovers below €50 million, account for 99 per cent of all German firms.

Ambitious and greedy are not the same thing. Will Arnold-Baker, ad agency start-up founder, said it was when they made their first few hirings of staff that they started to feel properly grown up and fulfilling their ambitions. Saatchi & Saatchi, the most dynamic advertising agency of the 1980s, launched their micro business in an office in Golden Square, in Soho, London (that 'golden' name was what they wanted). It's said that most of the office space was devoted to the reception and a presentation room. They allegedly employed actors to fill the place when potential clients came in. Their key was to seem bigger and more successful than they were. That's ambition. That's theatre. That's also marketing.

What no one talks about, but you need to know

Choosing exactly what to do matters less than you think

We want to blow the myth that the only way to go with a start-up is in tech. The tech space is overfilled with inflated expectations and whilst there are some great tech stories there are also some horror stories: *Airware*, a drone start-up, that burnt US $118 million. More disastrously, *Theranos*, with an allegedly breakthrough blood testing system, raised US $900 million (including US $150 million from Rupert Murdoch), was valued at US $10 billion in 2014 and zero in 2018. Founder Elizabeth Holmes was widely tipped to become the next Steve Jobs. Read *Bad Blood: Secrets and lies in a Silicon Valley startup* by Pulitzer prize winning writer John Carreyou, for the story in detail.

But it's not only tech that fails. *Juicero*, although they actually called themselves a tech juicer, was a machine that allegedly exerted 4 tonnes of pressure, but independent investigation showed you could juice just as well by squeezing the fruit in your hands.

Richard French, ex-Chairman of Y&R, serial advertising agency inventor and entrepreneur, is more relaxed about what you choose to do mattering less than why you choose to do it:

> I think in the end the thought of having to work for someone else was too awful to contemplate. Start anything. If it had not been an ad agency it might have been a bar, a sweet shop, a pedalo concession, an airline ... or just sitting on a hillside in the middle of France.

The funding problem...or is it?

The most poignant stories about funding we heard were from women who said they found the response, by the mostly male sources of money, were often quite hostile. Zana Nanu has a business called Gapsquare that has software designed to help clients understand, compare with benchmarks and close their gender pay gap. It's gone well and her clients include some well-known household names. She quotes Barclays Research, which says venture funds in tech start-ups by women account for only 2 per cent of all funding. She herself has had to bootstrap her business, which now has 11 employees. She recalls a meeting with a potential funder when she was told the following, 'Don't you have a man as Chairman? You should because then you'll be taken seriously'.

She's relaxed about all this saying that it avoids what she sees as a probable consequence to receiving funding from such sources, namely misogynistic intervention in the way that she runs the business.

In Poland no one seems to care about funding, with over half of all start-ups being self-funded. From our own experience we know that service businesses like advertising or PR can afford not to get embroiled with clueless money men. Of course they're not all clueless. Daniel Ross is the London point man for 'Yellow Woods', the investment vehicle for a wealthy South African family looking for worthwhile investments, often start-ups. His story of the average start-up is rather gloomy, but his diagnosis is accurate:

> [m]ost start-ups fail or miss targets and simply stagger on – absolute success or failure takes longer than you expect...often money runs out needlessly or relatively rich kids just lack the hunger or resilience to work at stuff.

The best source of money is called the 3Fs –'friends, family and fools'. Co-author Rachel Bell being neither a fool, maybe a friend but certainly family, has helped fund a start-up with her nephew Tom Hayward's business, an automotive, online, second-hand parts business called 'I Need Spares.com'. Her coaching has focused Tom on securing profit margin before growth and the results are impressive.

The potential for funders is huge, and as Peter Lederer, ex-Chairman of Gleneagles Hotel and now a serial entrepreneur reminds us, funding is much easier now than it was 10 years ago. But money alone is not enough. Start-ups need discipline and coaching too. As Will Arnold-Baker says, 'not many people know how to make money in business'.

Being top-boss for the first time isn't that easy

The thrill of not being at someone else's beck and call is offset by the discovery that what happens, or doesn't happen, is now all your fault. But in our experience, the smell of power is good and liberating. There's one big caveat. We should never behave like a corporate executive. We're a shopkeeper not a flashy CEO. John Hegarty, founder of BBH, the advertising agency, always called his large and thriving business in these terms when he said, 'I've got to get back to the shop'.

The thrill of not being at someone else's beck and call is offset by the discovery that what happens, or doesn't happen, now is all your fault.

The alpha male leader (or the Dinosaur Model as it should be called) is obsolete, but it still exists out there. One person we talked to said he was a hard task master. Sorry, we said, hard task masters belong to the past. Rightly so, the big buzz words now are, 'collaboration, inspiration and empathy'.

Being a boss doesn't mean being a bastard. It means being an inspiring leader and coach.

The crucial art of partnership: get on or get out

Choosing the right partner or partners is crucial. Going it alone is possible of course, but generally having someone, or several people, who complement our talents is better and more productive. In advertising Abbott Mead Vickers is the most successful start-up ever in advertising. David Abbott was recognized as the star, but the support, tolerance and kindness of his partners got the best out of David. The values were genuinely collectively felt and lived.

In our interviews all the businesses with several partners reflected on the difficulties of aligning ambitions, values and working styles. These are typical questions asked of us:

'How do you cope with a partner who's brilliant in meetings but is incredibly lazy?'

'How do you cope with someone obsessed with work–life balance and with little interest in growing the business?'

The answer is to take your time forming a partnership. Do not rush it. Never go into partnership without creating a prenup agreement. Be clear about what each of you wants. John Scott, who used to be HR Director of Lazard's Bank and who now runs Abune, a mediation business, describes a scenario he came across in which a very successful fast-growing business had two partners who, as time passed, started to get on each other's nerves. Neither quite knew why. But they were temperamental opposites and there was a chemical explosion. What had seemed complementary at one point, turned toxic and the business failed.

It's all about being grown up. Matt England, who started Sun Rum, began his entrepreneurial life developing Marie Rose Gin with a great friend. The relationship wobbled at work, so they split up, with his partner developing the gin brand on the one hand, and Matt developing a new rum brand on the other. They are still good friends.

Why some businesses fail and others thrive

Starting a business is thrilling. It's unlikely that we wouldn't want it to grow or that we wouldn't want people to admire it, but most of all we need to create and run a grown-up business, one that makes a profit and generates cash. What could go wrong?

There are six key reasons for success and failure.

I) HUNGER (OR LACK OF IT)

If we aren't hungry for success, starting a business is a bit like rushing into a great restaurant, grabbing the menu and then realizing we aren't hungry. Imagine it like this. Starting a business is like getting married, not something we'd take lightly, not something we'd do impulsively, but something we'd hope is going to last happily for a long time.

II) GETTING ON WITH PEOPLE AND PARTNERS

If we don't want to get on with people, we probably oughtn't to start a business. There are exceptions of course, like Kit Carruthers who has resolutely started the Ninefold Distillery on the Dormont Estate in Dumfries, Scotland, as a one-man band. But this is an add-on to the estate of which one day he'll be laird. Generally, start-ups thrive best when there's a solid partnership of complementary talents. The reason that many start-ups fail is because of relationship breakdowns. Sheri Roder, VP of Horizon Media in New York, remarks that (in general), 'men are to do with money; women are to do with relationships'. In the 2020s relationships are going to matter more because, increasingly, trust is more important than size and mere skill.

III) HAVING A BAD IDEA OR A BADLY MARKETED IDEA (OR BOTH)

Any idea well marketed can succeed (except in the tech world where for a product to have the smell of having been done before is a kiss of death). Often people spend months trying to be original and concoct an ingenious solution to a problem that no one actually has or, if they have, it's one they don't really care about. Better to be a very good web designer than a second rate advertising agency. Better to run a great café than an average restaurant. So, here's the mix that matters: success is going to depend 50 per cent on getting the product right and 50 per cent on getting the marketing right.

IV) MONEY: HAVING IT, MAKING IT AND USING IT

Bear in mind those wise words of Daniel Ross, 'too many people waste money needlessly'. In a start-up money is like water in a desert. Guard it. Be mean. Don't spend unless you have to. Those long, aimless, expensive lunches should be a thing of the past (but never underestimate the power of a productive 'working lunch' with an end in mind). Generally long walks and challenging conversations are more to the point. The liturgy of woes that start 'we simply ran out of money' can often be avoided by talking and keeping people in touch with all those good things you're doing.

V) 'DO YOU FEEL LUCKY PUNK?'

Clint Eastwood's words should get us replying, 'Yes, I feel lucky and confident'. We must like what we do and feel comfortable in our shoes. We should try to be excited about the world in which we live, become a compelling presenter and excite others. Let's hope we're confident and not cocky (that's a really shocking thing to be) and that we're happy. It matters how we feel, but more importantly it really matters how we *seem* to feel. Feel lucky. It shows you are optimistic and it's such a good vibe to give off.

VI) MANAGING AFFAIRS INCOMPETENTLY

John Eustace, who's advising the Portuguese Government on investing in and managing their entrepreneurial fund, describes his experiences of start-up managers, across all countries, as follows:

> There are lots of very bright people around who are poor managers of things, systems and people. They are wrapped in a bubble and need mentors and NEDs to help them keep their feet on the ground.

The most inexcusable reason for a business failing is from lack of attention, love or commitment. If we've decided to start something, whether it's a race, a game of monopoly or a business, the very least we can expect of ourselves is that we'll stick at it and try our best to be as good as we can at it.

Notes

1 A Black Swan is an unpredictable or unforeseen event, typically one with extreme consequences.

2 Digitally Native Vertical Brands like Billion Dollar Shave, Away luggage, Casper Mattresses and Lagom Kitchenware reinvent big markets by eliminating redundant margins in the distribution chain such as wholesalers or retailers. They tend to focus on high profit, lazy markets where market leaders are sitting back. This is where 'the disruptors' are waiting to pounce with energetic marketing and great products.

CHAPTER TWO

The start-up revolution

An overview

We live in a world of hyperbole and over-dramatization, so let's be careful about overclaiming here. Is this 'revolution', a blip, a trend or a genuine upheaval in the way things are working out? There are three perspectives from which to view what's going on:

I) FROM THE DEMOGRAPHIC PERSPECTIVE

Everything we are seeing right now suggests millennials, the middle-aged ex-executive and women with talent are scrutinizing the opportunities for going it alone very seriously. If we're in our late thirties and working for a big company, should we consider going it alone? The why-nots against doing it are quite serious. It's usually a money list: mortgage, educating and indulging our children, or our pleasant lifestyle that's the big inhibitor, followed by the terrors of letting everyone down by the possibility of failure. Many young people in our circle of friends flirted with taking the jump but at a time of maximum personal, financial exposure.

So, they held back; it just seemed so difficult. Now, however, people, in general, are more liberated in their thinking. We mustn't lack courage. If we have only a rustling of desire to do it, then we should do it. But we must plan how and when we do it and build a small war chest first to tide ourselves over. Because if we have the urge, the talent and the energy, we may possibly succeed and certainly have fun trying. But not by suddenly renouncing a monthly pay cheque without having enough spare cash to survive for six months or so.

We are going to consider the role of women specifically and in some detail. Their contribution to this book has been profound (and this is not only Rachel's influence). Across the board there's emerged a sense that winning doesn't need to be achieved just on men's terms or on conventional terms. There is no absolute need or divine imperative that a start-up must have perpetual double digit growth, that it must become market leader or that its founders must be swashbuckling pioneers. The great thing about running our own business is we write our own rules.

And women right now are doing just that.

II) FROM THE BIG BUSINESS PERSPECTIVE

Big businesses are watching what's going on in business right now in something resembling horror. Dr Sharon Varney at the Henley Business School is an expert on leadership and change. She says that whilst big companies have big money, they are hamstrung by conformity, process, risk aversion and a lack of creative thinking. All the fun is with the 'micro-mavericks'. Anyone in HR at any of the big companies is grappling with four things that are happening to them:

- It's very hard for big companies to recruit young graduate talent. If they get them in for an interview, these young people will tend to give the interviewers a hard time and quiz them on their corporate culture and on their record in dealing with sexual harassment and bullying. If they're in the food business they'll be antagonistic about the company's record with salt, sugar, palm oil and plastics.

- If they do persuade these young 'stars' to join, it's probable they'll walk out after a short while because the company won't be ready for their ethical standards or what they expect and demand of an employer. So, they'll be hard to recruit and hard to retain. This is happening worldwide. In Korea employers are tearing their hair out because, what they regard as sheer disobedience is, in fact, just the way the new generation is.
- Next, women are tending to return to their old job from maternity leave less often.
- And finally, after another round of right-sizing when the 'right' people are accepting voluntary redundancy, another bunch of 'emerging' talents suddenly resign to start up a new business that leaves a resource and talent gap.

McKinsey used to talk about 'the War for Talent'. Now there's a 'Chronic Talent Drain' with the best and the brightest leaving the ship because they believe that it's slowly sinking. *They also believe there's never been a better or more opportune time to start their own business, unfettered by old ideas.*

III) FROM THE CONSUMER PERSPECTIVE

Finally, the consumers, or more usefully the neighbourhoods in which we live, are talking about these trends because an increasing number of people they know are doing their own thing. Once a trend starts whereby people creating their own business in a start-up is seen as normal, exciting and desirable, momentum builds rapidly. And these neighbourhoods are becoming more anti-big corporation, berating them online for their many failings.

Someone once said, 'A bonfire starts at the bottom', which has the same kind of meaningless irrefutability as saying someone has to bury the undertaker. In fact, the fires of revolution are alight all over. There's never been a tougher time to hold a big, old, lazy business together or a better time to start a new, energetic, disruptive business, designed for the world we live in today.

A paradigm for the 2020s

The gin revolution

Gin used to be an old people's drink or a boring golf club beverage. Nothing could have been less cool. But a few years ago, a light switch was clicked and the off-licence shelves began to fill with new brands of gin. Gordons, Tanqueray, Bombay Sapphire were still there. Now, however, everyone seems to be making gin. David Gluckman, author of the important work on innovation, *That S*it Will Never Sell!*, and the inventor of many drink brands including Bailey's, Malibu and Singleton, is distinctly irritated by what he perceives as this indiscriminate riot of reckless innovation.

In 2013 there were 152 gin distilleries in the UK. In 2019 there were 315. There are well over 100 different gin brands, most of them relatively new to the market. With annual growth now running at over 25 per cent a year, sales of gin are projected to overtake scotch whisky by 2020. So, what on earth's going on?

The cost of entry is cheap. The gin you make today you can sell tomorrow (unlike whisky, which has to be barrelled and matured for years). Great packaging can dramatize a simple story (look at Kew Organic Gin, Explorer's Strength or Bathtub Gin). The pack designers are having a ball and doing an amazing job. And then there's Fever-Tree Tonic Water, another new disrupting brand that has set the bar for sector transformation, usurping brand leader Schweppes. Mixologists have seized on these exotic new gins as a cocktail base.

Finally, a lot of people earning huge salaries in the city decided to have some fun by being creative and doing something they really enjoyed...getting drunk, not just on any brand but on their own gin.

This is a revolution that has completely disrupted a dull old sector. What's happened to gin could happen anywhere. Whereas Innocent improved smoothies and Ben & Jerry's made much nicer ice cream, in gin it's been the perceptual reinvention of the whole sector. An epidemic of creativity infected a bunch of start-ups all at once. It's been like (in a very small way) an alcoholic Silicon Valley.

Helping start-ups to win

Four stories from people who help start-ups

All four are businesses focused on helping start-ups succeed. In the past starting a business meant you were on your own. This is no longer the case. Businesses like these are transforming the landscape and providing support systems that really make a difference.

YOU DON'T NEED A LAWYER, YOU NEED A FARILLIO

Merlie Calvert, who founded Farillio, is fast talking and, without ramming views down your throat, seems a mature millennial (she technically falls just outside this definition but is effortlessly surfing the millennial *zeitgeist*). She speaks simply and fearlessly. Here's what she writes about her Farillio business, which was formed at the beginning of 2017:

My latest adventure...Farillio.

Speedy. Easy. Law.

To help every small business with friendly, expert and affordable legal solutions is a significant ambition. We made it ours. And to be honest, we're obsessed with it.

'Better' to us means easier, faster, safer, more helpful and a lot more affordable – without ever compromising on the quality of our advisors or their expert advice.

She used to be a lead cellist in an orchestra, so being a team player comes naturally and is obviously fundamental. She graduated in law at Bristol University; went to S J Berwin as a trainee lawyer, then as a competition lawyer; and next at De Beers as Commercial Director.

She says she learnt more about being a lawyer when she was in a marketing role, where you fixed things fast and were unafraid of radical solutions. She also learnt to speak clear, simple English. It's a language called 'human' in a world where the *lingua franca* is a language known as 'jargon'.

She also has a sense of humour. Few lawyers seem to laugh much on the job, probably because chargeable time is too precious for laughter. At Farillio she is called Air Traffic Control not CEO. We think that's the way to go in a stuffy world. On the website she pitches their business winningly:

> We know first-hand how tough it can be to start out in business. We understand how not knowing, or having access to what you want, gets in your way. We understand how that wastes your time and costs way too much money. Almost all of us have founded at least one business before. Our experience tells us there's a better way to do business – simply, quickly, confidently and affordably.

In common with all marketing sceptics, we're cautious about believing 100 per cent in what people say about themselves, but this sounds just how Merlie speaks. In their unpretentious, open plan co-working offices in The Tech Hub, 101 Finsbury Pavements in the City of London, as evening draws in, Merlie talks about what she calls the 'new 20-year-old start-ups' who are in fact 40-year-olds, experienced in business but now on a start-up. They are surrounded by a community of fellow adventurers, and the spirit of collaboration prevents start-ups from that familiar feeling of 'floundering' because, quite simply, they're surrounded by like-minded people who are supporters and mentors.

Farillio feels like a pioneer with a vision of the future where great advice creates a community around itself, full of wisdom and compassion, attracting more and more to join the club.

GOOD MENTORING IS KEY FOR START-UPS: TURTLEWISE (CALIFORNIA)

If you want to be inspired, listen to Kevin Walker. From childhood he was taught to have a 'passion for learning'. Not just learning but also sharing that learning with others. In 2016 he started a digital mentoring company called TurtleWise, which is described on its website like this:

> TurtleWise is a frictionless mentoring system delivering 90 per cent of the benefits with 0 per cent of the hassle of coordinating in-person meetings...our patent-pending matching algorithm is part of our 'secret sauce'. Designed to mimic 'real-life', our community members are matched based on specific characteristics and attributes of an ideal advisor, chosen by the advice seeker.

Effectively it's a dating service between mentors and mentees. It's unique in creating a forum in which users can get mentoring help at any level. Like Farillio, it's low-cost and designed to help cash-challenged start-ups. Listening to Kevin's rich, avuncular voice, which is reminiscent of Morgan Freeman, is to experience three things – relaxation, trust and a desire to reveal one's thoughts. His wisdoms are expressed neatly:

'The world is so complicated you need to reach outside your network...'
'No one can tell you "*the answer*", but they can give you a "suite of solution sets"...'
'You must be true to yourself...'

He believes the power of mentoring, when done well, is that it allows you to reinvent yourself. This, of course, is precisely what we do in starting a new business. Before reinventing ourselves, he advocates the need to disengage (like we do when fixing a problem with our PC). Quite often, we do it by switching it off and switching it on again. It's the same with people. It's just that switching off seems quite hard for us to manage.

He says one thing about people that we like a lot, 'Human beings are big and little'. Mentoring is about bringing out our latent bigness whilst understanding it's often the little things that stop our greatness emerging.

CREATING A COMMUNITY OF ENTREPRENEURS
(PLATF9RM, BRIGHTON, UK)

It's called Platf9rm (not boring Platform9, mind, but Platf9rm – that's design for you) because there are only eight platforms at Brighton Station. So, here's the alternative to commuting. Seb Royle is the founder and inspiration. He started his working life at Regus, the multinational that provides office space, then set up Instant Offices Managed, which in due course he sold and moved the family to the seaside life of Brighton.

The experience in his two office sites compares favourably with trendy advertising agencies around the world – great, stylish, expensive furnishing; cheerful, light meeting areas; lots of smiling people; free coffee; free beer on Friday afternoons. Platf9rm is focused on making its 'members' (not co-workers) feel great. Seb has reimagined the personality of Brighton and expressed it in buzzy working and meeting spaces.

Brighton and Hove was nominated as one of Britain's 'Cities of the Future' in a study commissioned by HSBC. It was seen as booming in high tech, with a young demographic, emerging and vibrant creative industries and hosting major arts and music festivals. With a Premier Division Football Team and extensive infrastructure development, the 'City of the Future' seems more plausible. Platf9rm is a component in this changing reality, accelerating the probabilities of success by making co-working a pleasure as well as functionally effective.

Platf9rm is an example of how the world is changing. The thing most likely to make a start-up business be still-born is for entrepreneurs to work on it on their own in a chilly garret. The art of sharing, and feeling that we're part of a flourishing community, is not new but in an increasingly bureaucratic and commuter-driven world we talk less, are often smartphone and laptop imprisoned and have lost the knack of relaxing around a coffee machine. Yuval Noah Harari in his 2011 book *Sapiens* identifies one of the key drivers in the rapid development of *Homo Sapiens* as our ability and desire to gossip and exchange ideas.

In an increasingly bureaucratic and commuter-driven world we talk less, are often smartphone and laptop imprisoned and have lost the knack of relaxing around a coffee machine.

So, the idea of Platf9rm is not new. It really started around 200,000 years ago.

WORLD CLASS INCUBATION IS THE WAY TO GET READY TO WIN: SETSQUARED BRISTOL

The SETsquared Partnership of five incubators, linked to the Universities of Bristol, Bath, Exeter, Southampton and Surrey, was rated the best incubator at the World Incubation Summit in Toronto March 2018. This is what Monika Radclyffe, the Centre Director of SETsquared Bristol, says about why she thinks they're so highly rated, 'We take things seriously here – no beanbags and milk shakes...people want to work not do frothy Google type stuff...we're a bit more grown up than that'.

What Monika and her team are doing is pretty remarkable at SETsquared. What originally started as a government initiative 16 years ago, is currently working in Bristol with 83 start-ups, all in the tech space.

Their key aim is to prepare start-ups to be 'investment ready'. SETsquared coaches them in how to create the presentation material that will inform and impress, together with an understanding of what funders are looking for. They work together on plans, back-up material to the plans, strategies and 'exits'. Yes, well we know how rude I've been about the 'exit' word, but Monika patiently explains that this is the tech space where speed of success is absolutely critical (no exit plan equals no funding potential).

She says that funding is not really a problem because SETsquared has a huge network of funders and a track record for making sure their incubated start-ups are investment ready when they are introduced to potential funders. So, whilst success is not assured, a presentation should never fail through being ill thought out or short on detail.

Monika describes the sort of people who are in the incubator. Idealists, of course, people who want to change the world, to which she adds this – a healthy corrective to romantic idealism – you need a successful business platform to change the world because 'changing the world is not a hobby'. But money in the early start-up phase is neither mentioned nor thought about. This is fascinating. It isn't until the final moments of investment readiness that money – so often a distraction, if prematurely discussed – gets considered.

Monika is pragmatic, not least when reflecting on the challenges start-ups often experience – loneliness, fluctuating self-confidence (she is focused on the big mental health issues in taking that start-up plunge), a tendency towards tunnel vision and a failure to visualize the bigger picture. And she gently acknowledges the experience gap many face, 'they don't know what they don't know – these are very young people with more enthusiasm than experience'. But she is very strict about cocky young entrepreneurs if they are unwise enough to cross swords with her. 'We clear out people with massive egos...we can't be wasting our time with that sort of thing.'

SETsquared takes their start-up candidates on an intense and exacting journey with great mentoring and expert technical business advice. The programme and the process seem exactly what is needed everywhere in the UK.

Perspectives and stories

Setting out to change the world (a little)

As Monika Radclyffe says, 'this is not a hobby'.

So far, we've shown the importance of having the proper advice, finding the right community to share ideas with, and being mentored and guided to pitch your business to maximum effect to help provide a good, grown-up start to being a proper start-up. We're going to examine some examples of younger start-ups to see how they've done it, made mistakes, learnt and moved on. But before that, a few words from John Scott, ex HR Chief at Lazard's Bank, then PwC where he ran the HR team in their Middle Eastern business, and next decided to walk the Appalachian Trail in the United States (2,200 miles). People die doing this. People get attacked by bears. People go crazy with the loneliness and their sore feet. 'Why?' we ask him:

> Because it's there…because I wanted to see what it was like… because I wanted to see how it changed me…most of all I wanted to get closer to big nature not just strolling on a Sunday.

The Appalachian Trail is the hiker's equivalent of space travel. John now has his own mediation business. In business, minor disputes can escalate, but often they can be settled quickly at low cost employing a mediator rather than by rushing off to a large legal practice. John is focused on two things in the autumn of his working life. First common sense. Second, simplicity. We all have too much stuff. Too many bits of paper, too much choice and, accordingly, too much confusion. Keeping it simple is great advice. Remember Ronald Reagan's line 'if you're explaining you're losing'. Here's John not quite explaining, rather more declaiming:

> In this increasingly complex, kick-arse, hurtling, over-provided world most people want a simpler life. To all potential start-ups I ask them to consider if their product and business model is as simple as it could be. Because – in a complex world simplicity sells.

He's involved in a successful (simple) start-up. Fishbox. They deliver fresh, sustainable fish and shellfish direct to your door or desk within 48 hours of being landed. All fish is freshly caught from Scottish waters. He's also involved with Farillio. No, neither is a unicorn concept, but both are simple, sensible and they work.

Start-up stories from millennials

How these young start-ups feel, think and behave

This is not, neither was it ever intended to be, a quantitative study: plenty of those exist already. This is about getting inside the heads of a group of talented young people to see what we can learn from them and what experiences they've gone through that may allow those who follow them to short-cut some of the tasks in starting a new business. More interesting than 'how to do it' – although we'll address that – is to examine the hopes and fears, the feelings and the stuff that people normally don't tell you. Let's start by quoting the legendary advertising guru David Ogilvy and what he said about researching people. It's this truth, it's this paradox that makes us love the human race and the late Ogilvy's thinking so much (quoted variously by Rory Sutherland – *Alchemy,* and John Haidt – *The Righteous Mind*): 'People don't think what they feel, don't say what they think and don't do what they say'.

What's the driving motive of young start-ups?

We talked to people who set up businesses in cold brewed coffee, alcohol-free ale, teaching, online further education, a rock band, a car parts business, a media venture, social entrepreneurial projects, a professional services business, a tech solution to locating confused old people. What do they have in common? All of them have set up these businesses before the age of 34.

There are no dramas here. No moments of epiphany. Three discovered their attraction to running their own business whilst at university. Two started in 'career' jobs after graduating and then tasted freedom when given a project outside the normal hum drum of their 'proper' job. Two pursued their passions whilst at school...one through university, one avoiding university. Two in educational businesses, one through passion, one through rational scrutiny of the options, having done a spell at two big businesses. One through seeing a gap in a market and then having a flash of insight.

What's it been like?

Hugh Duffie is Australian and believes in cold brewed coffee in the way that people in bookshops believe in great literature or wine shops believe in fine wine. He is a connoisseur. It's been tough. It's been about sleeping on people's couches and doing three jobs to survive. Tough? Yes, but it's been fun too, especially when his brand Sandows appeared on *The Great British Bake-Off* in 2014. Hugh is very focused, determined and really believes in his product.

Chris Hannaway went to Bath University, reading Business Administration. That was fun, 'we even got to go on trips to Iceland and Edinburgh and when we were told to go on two six month placements, I managed to persuade them I should go on one of those placements with myself developing a new product'. It strikes me Chris is a pretty good salesman if he could do this. He's phlegmatic about problems and upbeat about his world. He started 'Infinite Sessions' a 0 per cent abv ale with his brother. Both are keen sportsmen and health fanatics. 'We love beer but more the taste than the buzz.' He loves freedom, momentum and change. He's in a hurry.

Raphael Ferrer Sánchez studied Computer Science at university in Spain and whilst there founded a company called Neki through which he invented a wearable location finder. Originally designed as a bracelet for small children, he eventually changed it to a location finder for the elderly and confused. He was always going to do this, working for himself and not working for a corporate. He's patient, resilient and relaxed. He says it's been fun and rewarding. He's flying.

Vicki Harrocks is not quite a start-up, but with her MA in 'Making Performance' from Edge Hill University in the UK, her work with the children's theatre company 'Another Planet Productions' and her freelance choreographic and dance teaching she takes us to a new enterprising place – theatre. She loves what she does, especially in inspiring and bringing out the best in children. She's enthralling in the way she talks about her life. Life for her and her pupils seems like a wonderful ballet. With her classes, she's creating start-ups of the future.

Kit Carruthers has a PhD in Carbon Capture and Storage but is also heir to being laird on the family estate at Dormont in Dumfries, Scotland. He's dreaming of generating extra income by setting up a distillery producing 'Ninefold Rum'. Not any old rum. The best rum ever. He probably will, given his thoroughness.

Al Taylor is on his fourth start-up. He worked for McKinsey after university and before the age of 30 started a new business, 'Workplace Dynamics', which conducted employee surveys at over 4,500 companies each year assessing their organizational health. This was sold for a good sum. Al is pragmatic. What he does is 'a job but without a safety net'. The thrill of starting a business takes a distant second place to family, mortgage, educational fees and stuff like that. It struck us he was very well organized.

Tom Maynard's car broke down. As a DIY technician he was shocked by how much it cost, how long it took and how grisly the customer experience was in getting the necessary replacement spare part. So, he set up his online business 'I Need Spares. com'. Now two years later it's growing and making a good margin.

George Rendel went into publishing and consultancy at two good and respected businesses, Pearson and Accenture, after leaving university. But, 'at the back of my mind starting a business had always seemed a cool thing. The trouble with big corporations is you're always so remote from the bottom line'. George is a self-confessed workaholic. This hard work is paying off in a successful start-up, 'The Career Portal', under which are two portals for aspiring medics and lawyers. A new product focused on STEM subjects was launched in 2019.

Daisy Stapley-Bunten has started a magazine *The Start-Up Magazine*. She had this insight, 'a lot of people come out of university looking for a perfect job doing what they love', but they're thwarted by the grind of corporate life unless they do their own thing. She's inspired by the way markets work now, changing from consumer bases to communities of users. On a personal level she's driven by an ambition to succeed, 'if you know what you want and are hungry enough, you'll get it'.

Hannah Philp is a social entrepreneur who says, 'I've never felt there wasn't a problem I couldn't tackle and solve'. After university she spent seven years in investor relations and as Marketing Director of an investment trust learning all the stuff she needed in this capitalist world. Since then she's founded 'Her Stories', using the arts to support marginalized women and being on the Development Board of the 'Women's Trust' helping young women trapped in poverty. She's also now setting up a co-working space for women start-ups in Dalston.

Finally, a would-be rock star, drummer Harry Maitland. He describes the keys to creating his first band 'Basement Effect' as follows (he's now with the Liverpool Indie band 'Rats'):

1 **Awareness.** Creating a torrent of pictures and music earning 'likes' on social media.
2 **Sampling.** Busking for long spells (it earned them £2,000 a day).
3 **Reputation.** Using 'likes' on social media to justify being signed up for 'proper' gigs.

He utterly loves what they do (especially being a supporting act to 'Happy Mondays'). Engaging a really big crowd, he says, is unbelievably addictive and thrilling.

What's gone right for them?

What always goes most right is the sound of applause, the clink of money or the surge in support. But it isn't just success that ticks the box. Creating new things that work, like Hannah's start-ups do, enjoying your own product like Hugh and Chris do, and seeing and feeling something that you've created is great like Daisy, Vicki and Harry have. They own their own achievements.

For all, apart from George and Al, the money is a peripheral issue. They are all business-like people, but underlying all of these start-ups is a determination to survive and a love of what they do. But beyond survival and passion for their invention there's one word they use which defines a potentially winning business: momentum.

What's gone wrong?

Big stuff. Hugh has diluted his equity because he had to eat. Chris's first venture 'Arctic Farm', a frozen yoghurt, was copied and in effect stolen from him. His view about this is a very mature *c'est la vie*. Rafa's first two versions of 'Neki' failed in the market in terms of sales despite positive research (read that David Ogilvy quote, 'people don't do what they say'). Kit Carruthers says he knows nothing about marketing and that this is beginning to stress him (and so it should – find someone to help you Kit).

Harry, George and Al have all had partnership/team issues to sort out and have sorted them. Well done, because people are complex. You can't expect them to see things like you do. They aren't always reliable. What they've all recognized is a great idea plus brilliant marketing, but with a less than optimal relationship with people you work with, could impede success.

Biggest disappointment?

Strangely there were very few 'I really wish I hadn't done that' moments. Hugh's equity dilution is one. Vicki's disappointment with the educational establishment's attitude towards the arts and her concern about the long-term damage this will do to the economy, is another. George's disappointment is worth considering specifically, especially as it resonates with our own personal experiences. He wishes those around him worked harder, were as committed and focused on giving 100 per cent to the task. Sorry George, most people don't work as hard as we do. Grit your teeth and carry on doing what you do. We did.

Biggest (useful) learning?

When Tom Hayward first stumbled on that great insight, that the value of the spare parts on a written-off car was so high, he set up his first business in an open air site alongside a vehicular graveyard. This was great and seemed sensible except he was driven out of business before you could blink by the local council as though, as he put it, he was a 'gypsy grave robber'.

He next set up in office premises with an eat-your-lunch-off-the-floor spotless warehouse. 'Ineedspares.com' has a smart website too. Hayward (Founder and Managing Director) describes the aim of his business thus on his LinkedIn site:

> [t]o streamline the recycling process from End-Of-Life-Vehicles through to the retail of Green Parts by means of technology, automation and e-commerce.

Lesson: A smart façade seems to suggest a smarter business and appeases officials who are rather easily impressed by appearances.

How confident do they feel now?

Each of these entrepreneurs is past that 'dangerous – still on life-support' phase. Their confidence is most likely to be underpinned by their own sense of momentum. Hugh's worried about not growing fast enough. Chris got into Tesco at the end of 2018. Al and George are doing brilliantly.

Overall, six are movers and shakers and none is lacking in momentum. They all deserve to succeed and almost certainly will.

Millennial magic

Above all, millennials are optimists – not all of them of course will succeed and we still have that warning from the Prince's Trust ringing in our ears about how stressed they are. Stressed by exams, peer group expectations and the draining effects of too much social media. Interestingly, the youngest of our interviewees has cut out social media from his personal life (not his business life) because, he says, it's so incredibly time-wasting.

The important thing we are finding is that the desire for money, lots and lots of it, is pretty well missing from millennials.

The important thing we are finding is that the desire for money, lots and lots of it, is pretty well missing from millennials. The traps that constrained many baby boomers from being more entrepreneurial (mortgages, owning nice cars) is missing in their simplified lives. All the available research data shows their purchases and brand preferences are based on quality. But not on quantity. Two pairs of jeans are enough. What these millennials most need is great mentoring from people who can open their receptive minds even wider and who can help them distil their thinking and ambitions. Walk into Platf9rm or Huckletree West, the White City co-working space (or its five other sites in London), and the spirit of learning and listening can be strongly felt.

Ruth Rochelle, a leading executive coach, disputes our view that there's a positive responsiveness to change in today's world. She says as a race, humanity talks bravely but scuttles into a corner when real change happens. Millennials are certainly much more nimble, aided by the fact that many are more likely now to be setting their own rules rather than being an employee. Ruth also raises an interesting aside on the consequences of scaling up:

> The difference between start-up and scale up is very acute...this is partly because of the arrival of heavyweight, traditional investors (at this stage). Money (especially a large amount of it) changes everything. Idealism takes a kicking.

Start-up stories from women

Women worry about relationships, men about transactions and money

One of the more successful books has been the 2002 title *Why Men Don't Listen and Women Can't Read Maps* by Alan and Barbara Pease. It tells a story of how women and men have different values and different sets of norms. We know that only 6 per cent of FTSE 100 CEOs are women, that only 2 per cent of funding in the tech space goes to women entrepreneurs, and that data clearly shows female-led businesses tend to grow slower than men's. So, women are far from having it their own way. Some men have pointed at the relative failures of Marissa Mayer ex CEO of Yahoo, Carly Fiorina ex CEO of Hewlett Packard and even (unfairly) Harriet Green ex CEO of Thomas Cook, as examples of how, with very few examples, women aren't cut out for the battleground of business. Professor Elisabeth Kelan, who specializes in studying women leaders, describes the increasing trend towards 'Mumpreneurs', where the continuum is: *university>graduate trainee>rising executive>maternity>start-up*.

The deterrents to returning to corporate life after maternity leave are diverse. There's the hassle of growth and the blind quest for wealth; the exhaustion of corporate politics and the competing for advantage; the noise and the self-importance of it all and of course the aching fear of failure. (In a telephone interview with me in 2018, Sheri Roder, VP at Horizon Media New York, described the devastating effect losing a job, once in the past, had had on her, saying that she probably took it much more personally than a man would have done.)

Elisabeth Kelan in an interview and in her articles in *The Times* has discussed the 'glass cliff' – the trend of putting women into impossibly hard and precarious roles and blaming them (as women) if it fails or praising the astuteness of the men in hiring her (if it succeeds). There have been for some time a set of behaviours encouraged by men and submitted to by women that perpetuate the myth that women fail more often (they don't) or are less committed (they aren't).

Particularly good news for women, perhaps surprisingly, lies in China, where in 2018 they had 102 self-made female billionaires, two-thirds of the world total (Block, 2019). And Chinese women entrepreneurs are twice as 'successful' as their male counterparts, according to Rupert Hoogewerf, Chairman, *Hurun Global Self-Made Women Billionaires List* (Brinded, 2019).

What women are doing is changing the game there, in the United States and everywhere. They are going out on their own and writing the rules on their own terms. They are not hiring women exclusively to work for them, but corporate alpha males are getting short shrift from them. The prophecies of Tom Peters back in 2001 have been a long time coming. He cites the Deloitte problem of being great at hiring high-performing women and, then, better still at losing them because of its male-dominated culture, so much so that many had simply switched professions. Fortunately, since the early 2000s, Deloitte has changed.

Quite simply it's not just women but their essential values that are prevailing now amongst most people in business and especially with millennials.

Women: some new start-up winners and thinkers

Sheri Roder was a talented young Marketing Development Director at Diageo in the UK. She's now Executive Vice President at Horizon Media in New York and co-founder of Limitless, a women's leadership initiative in New York. She thinks the trick is not to have women-only businesses but to help men and women to work better together. Specifically, to get men more relationship focused.

Lisa Matthews has a master's and a PhD in Engineering and had a senior job with Arup for 11 years, developing entrepreneurial expertise in the firm, especially in the digital space. She then became a consultant for several years. Now she's co-developed Helly Hobby, a company creating life-engine technology that gives machines the ability to think about time the way humans do. Her product 'Our Canary' helps people organize their chaotic, busy lives.

Sharon Varney is a consultant at the Henley Business School and is an expert on leadership and change. She runs lots of workshops and laments the trends that scale seems to create. More conformity, predictability, more process and less thinking. She loves mavericks, radicals and start-ups. She is convinced our future, as a race, lies in maverick creativity.

Zara Nanu is the founder of Gapsquare, the system that helps businesses close the gender pay gap. She has a PhD and her academic background is focused on human rights and social justice. She stood as a local politician in parliamentary elections in Bristol more to provide herself with a platform than in believing it was possible for her to win. We'll be hearing a lot more of her.

In Africa women are increasingly making the running. The problem they face is a legacy of bureaucracy and corruption. Magatte Wade, Mayor of Meckhe, a 30,000 population town in Senegal, is an angry woman. She rages about the streams of people trying to leave Africa. She's also an entrepreneur who says the solution is easy – 'just make it easy to start a business and do business'.

Amy Armstrong is what author Malcolm Gladwell called a maven…a person who creates networks and by so doing makes things happen. One of the most successful Area Managers of Learn Direct, she now powers her way through life linking talent to talent. She describes herself as a transformative wellbeing and leadership coach. She spends a lot of her time encouraging start-ups.

Becky Sage is CEO of Interactive Scientific, working on digital tools for the EdTech and pharmaceutical market (especially in the area of VR). As well as being a leading gymnast and an actress, she is driving a successful tech business with energy and a sense of discovery.

Margorita Kolton (known as 'Gosha') was previously the Managing Director of Tetra Pak Poland. She is now running her own business as a business mentor, mainly with start-ups. She says it's relatively easy to get going because there's still considerable growth in the market and people are focused on sales rather than on getting funding (since bootstrapping is normal). Women in Poland account for around a third of start-ups. She is confident of the future for Poland and its women entrepreneurs.

Poppy Szkiler is the grand-daughter of John Connell, founder of the UK's Noise Abatement Society. After an acting career on British television, she founded Quiet Mark in 2011 as a regimen for testing products for their quietness and awarding the quietest with a QM seal of approval. They now work with around 50 major brands including John Lewis, Dyson and Samsung. They've also launched the brand into the United States and Germany.

Kati Byrne (and her partner) have set up a business called 3dify – a 3D business that can create small 3D body scans quickly. They did this when they launched the business in a slot on *BBC TV* with Bill Thompson the technology writer. Kati is a creative PR person and her partner, Ian, was Head of Multimedia for Rupert Murdoch's News International. Theirs is a business that explores how to commercialize 3D imaging at low cost. They are exploring the future.

Rachel Melsom appears later in the book as one of the most interesting 'pivot heroes' we've discovered. But she also has significant start-up experience. After an early career in advertising, media (Virgin and CBS) and PR (as a partner at Brunswick), she started and sold an IPR and a media business.

Elisabeth Kelan is Professor of Leadership and Organisation at Essex Business School, Essex University. She was previously at Cranfield and King's College London. *The Times* has featured her as one of the management thinkers to watch, and her research findings and her insights are regularly reported in the media. She keeps a keen eye on the role of women in a changing world, especially in the start-up arena.

Ruth Rochelle has earned a big reputation as a partnership fixer in several big companies in the marketing services and creative sector and, especially, start-ups moving to scale-ups. She founded and has been running her company, Creation, for 20 years. She describes its role as liberating creative power, building productive relationships, positively transforming leadership and effective teamwork. She has saved partnerships in start-ups from foundering and, as such, can give valuable insights.

How these female entrepreneurs think, feel and behave

Their focus is on three things: culture, mission and interpersonal relationships. The success of their ventures is unlikely to hang just on a great idea, a marketing insight or something that derives from external factors; their concentration is on internal structural, strategic and behavioural issues and on building a business with strong foundations and values. Whereas quite a lot of men seem comfortable in focusing on tactics, nearly all the women we've talked to are concentrating on the destination, the strategic aim, not just the journey itself.

There was remarkably little hyperbole in the way they talk about business. They are quite practical and patient. Lisa Matthews said this:

> I'm sceptical about so much of the start-up mythology. It's easy to do things fast but really hard to do the right things. That takes time. Priority one is not that business plan that the bro culture embraces.

And this feels right. It sounds like a 21st-century business professional thinking aloud, as opposed to a fast-buck 'entrepreneur'. The key words are *sceptical* – good word, not enough positive scepticism around; *hard to do the right things* – yes, but that's what matters; *takes time* – we live in impatient times; and men, especially, are into *speed decision making* and that put-down of business plans that is long overdue. Very often the worst businesses have the best business plans. Enron, Carillion, Patisserie Valerie – we bet they all had wonderful business plans.

What's their driving motive?

Cecilia Thirlway, ex-Civil Servant and now starting her own business, pointed out the difficulties of being a woman entrepreneur. Somehow, she said, when a woman talks about setting up her business, men often seem to think she'll be producing 'homemade bunting' and that she's being underwritten by her husband. The 'enterprising self' is a myth, so long as women's voices aren't being heard. But we think that's only partly true and that the dam of scepticism is being breached because increasingly smart women are doing smart things.

Zara and Poppy have seized an opportunity and a problem (respectively gender pay inequality and the increasing noise in our lives) and through sheer determination, self-belief and a conviction that their cause is right and urgent, have turned their solution to the problem into important businesses. Years back, when Poppy started, she was battling men whose desire was for that 'business plan' not a crusade. But a crusade is what Poppy produced and today Quiet Mark is a big global idea.

What's it been like?

What has struck us both – unsurprisingly – is how hard women work at getting it 'right'. In *A Whole New Mind* Daniel Pink says:

> The keys to the kingdom are changing hands. The future belongs to a very different kind of person with a very different kind of mind – creators and empathizers, pattern recognizers and meaning makers.

All the women we've talked to get this. This is definitely not a 'hobby' as far as they're concerned; the word 'fun' is not much used. They have great resilience and are sensible about how to be effective, displaying what Margaret Heffernan describes as essential qualities in her 2008 book, *Women on Top*:

> To be innovative over the long term requires stamina. Not burnout. Not macho displays of overwork...good ideas rarely come in the middle of an all-night work session; they're more likely to come when driving home. To be able to improvise effectively, the brain has to stay fresh. 'Staying Power' isn't just about not quitting; it's about true mental stamina.

Dr Becky Sage empathizes with this saying that, as so much of the work Scientific Interactive does is in 3D, she's always thinking in 3D – which is rather tiring.

Katy Paul-Chowdhury in Toronto says developing her business, as a writer, has become easier as she's no longer tyrannized by a lack of money. Whenever we hear someone say that, and because being tyrannized by money can be so hideously dispiriting, we think of the then-skint J K Rowling scribbling in an exercise book creating one of the greatest entertainment start-ups of all time, *Harry Potter*.

Kati Byrne says it isn't the workload, it's the sheer abundance of ideas they've had that makes her life stressful. Like having too many apples in an orchard. The 3D space is very PR-able, but what she hasn't reconciled herself to is the idea of building a big business and being trapped into recruiting people and having the responsibility for, in effect, feeding their families. But 3D is fast moving and changing and probably not a place for empire building.

Lisa Matthews says despite the struggles and the time that it's taken getting the basics in the Our Canary business right, she feels good about the process they've been through. The concept is a system of household organization to save us all from messing up: 'A single place for juggling the never-ending jigsaw puzzle that is working family life' is how it's described.

Amy Armstrong says mentoring and surrounding yourself with talent in a co-working hub, or whatever it takes to learn and share, is key. The mountains people have to climb can be vertiginous, like someone in one of her workshops who was going from employing just one person to hiring up to 10 interns within the following three weeks, never having managed anyone before. As Lisa Matthews would have said, 'stop – wait – think'.

The journeys have been embarked upon with thoroughness and good spirits. As Cecilia Thirlway put it, 'the knack of being happy is too often missing in the debate about work'. Earlier we said the word fun was not much used, but we've since detected something more solid than that. Quiet, contented satisfaction.

What's gone right?

When studying the businesses of women entrepreneurs and start-ups, there was, with one exception, a solid sense of getting by and competent survival and, at the best, very satisfactory growth. The one exception was someone in video production who had done a pivot from this disrupted commoditized business. The list of lessons was:

- These were a series of businesses setting off with harmonious purpose and a commitment to brilliant execution.
- Nearly everyone is trying out micro now. Sharon Varney observed 'hobby businesses' being set up on the side by executives in 'Monster Corporations'. At Clear-Score, for instance, executives are positively encouraged to 'go entrepreneurial'. We love the idea of working on a complex fintech spreadsheet and being interrupted by a peer saying, 'will you buy some of my ice cream?'
- That 'voice' that women have historically lacked, is beginning to be heard. The voice is not revolutionary nor even particularly disruptive. It's quietly determined. And it's a voice that speaks to the people who do the work and make the real difference. It is a voice of calm collaboration that will be increasingly intolerant of the old fashioned management styles that drove businesses of the past.

That 'voice' that women have historically lacked, is beginning to be heard. The voice is not revolutionary nor even particularly disruptive. It's quietly determined.

These developments will lead to a better, less turbulent, but no less creative world.

Biggest disappointments

The biggest disappointment is always people. People who fail to play as team members, people who don't try hard enough or aren't flexible enough. Ruth Rochelle, the mentor, regards Robert Kegan, a Development Psychologist at Harvard as something of a role model. He writes in an article in *Executive Inspiration* called 'Uncovering your Immunity to Change':

> We have to be relaxed that most people don't see the world through new-world lenses...what blocks us from changing are very often deeply ingrained cultural assumptions.

But the disappointment isn't just about the way people behave, it's about the way money is perceived by some. If you are a funder or investor in a business, money takes priority. There's this irony whereby the money is primarily controlled by men – banks, VCs, funds – whilst increasingly the start-ups are started by women. This paradox leads to the biggest disappointment of all.

Despite what the pundits say, the relationship between men and women in business has changed less than seems credible. The slow speed of change, especially when it comes to funding, is very strange, but women are not complaining, they are circumventing and they're bootstrapping. Interestingly, in developing countries, investors prefer to invest with women as they are seen as being more reliable, prudent and patient with the money lent to them. Here's what an angel investor in India, Nikunj Sha, said in response to our comments about female talent in the UK:

> Women (here) work harder and those who make it are amazing partly because they've had so much to overcome. Nearly all the people I employ in my executive search business in Mumbai are women because they're better.

Biggest (useful) learning

Kirstin Furber makes a useful observation:

> It's team-fit that new-wave businesses are particularly obsessed about. Because it's teams not individuals who'll make businesses fit for purpose in the complex 2020s and beyond. Interestingly diversity of interest is prized above focus and single minded dedication.

Our world of communication has shifted from telling to engaging and entertaining. In her business, the law, Merlie Calvert says this is essential, otherwise people switch off. Ruth Rochelle warns the big corporates that new-wave women simply won't tolerate the old business models. She tells the story of a very successful fintech in which the talented mid-twenties women are (in effect) working together in the business in a kind of parallel organization...that's one step short of a start-up.

How confident do they feel?

They're pretty confident really and much more in control of their lives too. But from our sample we detect something else important. The women are ambitious but not driven in a bleeding-steak go-and-kill-them-cowboy way. For most the key is to build, develop and grow a business with great values and a balanced approach to life.

Margaret Heffernan (again) quotes a start-up success led by a woman called Carol Latham who was divorced, broke and who set up a profitable high-tech business called Thermagon in the United States, first schooling and then employing inner-city neighbours, many of whom spoke little English. 'You can create value out of nothing with people just by giving them a chance to prove themselves.'

When you read that you feel the same quality of hope we derived from listening to all these entrepreneurs.

Start-up stories from experienced executives

Second generation start-ups

The accepted wisdom is we get more content as we get older. This may have been true before those millennials started to flex their muscles. Now we're not so sure. But what we see in our middle-aged start-ups (for this I'm talking 40- to 60-year-olds) is a focus and circumspection that their younger counterparts can't match. Each concentrates on where they can achieve most lever-age, most impact and make some money too.

Experience is like that lustrous shine on wood that is acquired over time, with effort and a repetitive process. Whilst millennials don't know what they don't know, the middle-aged do know what they don't know, which sometimes makes them more cautious and averse to unnecessary risk.

Whilst millennials don't know what they don't know, the middle-aged do know what they don't know, which sometimes makes them more cautious and averse to unnecessary risk.

Their downside is that most of them may have been locked into a corporate bureaucracy, playing the business political game, often with great skill. They may find it hard to forget the regimen. They may have become used to the bad habits: getting up too early, going to bed too late, drinking too much, eating out a lot, seeing their family and friends too seldom, travelling on transatlantic or transcontinental flights frequently.

That middle-aged itch

We've encountered three specific groups of 'middle-aged' entrepreneurs:

1 Those fleeing, with eyes wide open, from the well-paid comfort and complacency of a senior executive role into the freedom, but discomfort of a new start-up.
2 Those finding themselves doing something new and different but without quite the 'this is what I was really meant for' zeal.
3 Those doing something new from a position of retirement, or as a hobby, that may then turn into a business. This third group is lucky in not having had to defer to a corporate boss for some time. Their second careers are as much for fun as money, but they will be approached with professional rigour, nonetheless.

The first and second groups are more interesting and represent a more important development. This is as much to do with the difficulties facing the big, legacy businesses as the importance of this new climate of enterprise we are seeing on the increase.

The pluses of life in the big company are obvious. The culture of the club, especially in or close to the C-suite, can be intoxicating. Even the politics can be thrilling. Meeting people at work from all over the world, possibly eating and drinking together, celebrating success, all this is pleasant. Basking in the feeling of being in an invincible team is inspiring. The money is good, the perks are good, and the ride is exhilarating.

But...and this is a big BUT...the fun wears thinner as you get older, as the divide between millennials and generation X widens, especially in tech competence, with colleagues speaking what feels like an alien, new language and having a more acute perception of the nuances of new-generation behaviour. All of this can make being 50 feel rather old. In reality, at 50, both men and women have on average 30+ years left to live, whereas 50 years ago it was just 20 or less years. Today's 50-year-old is only halfway through their adult life. And what was once considered banter, suddenly becomes bullying as the economic climate gets tougher and old-fashioned 'humour' disappears from the workplace.

There is a way, of course, which is to take a sabbatical, but, in these uncertain times, companies are nervous about ideas like this. Roger Alexander, the former Chairman of Lewis Silkin and Partners, the legal firm, went on one many years ago and described to me his astonishing sense of rebirth and clarity of thinking that came from it.

And there are caveats, let's face it, in going out on your own, whether alone or with a partner and partners. As Al Taylor so beautifully put it, 'it's a job but without a safety net'. The competitive world is brutal and somehow more confrontational and crueller without the insulation of a big company. Everything takes longer than you expect or need. The lack of resource can be shocking, especially when the lavatory's blocked and now it's *your* job to fix it, not that of maintenance. You can suffer from wavering self-confidence, loneliness and feeling shabby. Adam Spence said a grubby office and dress-down clothes reduced his sense of self-worth for a while.

Changing the world and creating a new life is not a hobby. The buck stops with you. But that buck is more exciting than a monthly salary cheque.

But there is an upside. It's your challenge, you own it, it's 'your shop' and winning is worth the pain and tastes much sweeter than it ever did in a big company. Monika Radclyffe, MD of SETsquared, takes it very seriously, and she's right. Changing the world and creating a new life is not a hobby. The buck stops with you. But that buck is more exciting than a monthly salary cheque. It really is.

How these mature entrepreneurs think, feel and behave

THE LIGHTBULB QUARTET (FOUR WHO SIMPLY *HAD* TO DO A START-UP)
Adam Spence, co-founder of Edition Capital in 2016, would be irritated to be called middle-aged as he was born only around 1980. He could only be considered a 'mature' start-up having put in time, qualifying to be an accountant and then spending seven years at Ingenious. Starting his business was hard and quite uncomfortable. He hated fudging stuff that he didn't really understand, having no money, living in a Soho, London, hovel of an office. It was indescribably dreary. Then business picked up and that seminal experience of hiring people changed everything. They can see success now and the partners still own 80 per cent of the business. It's not entirely easy – business seldom is and partnerships often even less so.

Matthew Bellringer had 17 years in IT, 13 of these at Sussex University, UK. Before he resigned, he headed the team running Microsoft-related services on the campus, responsible for 8,000 endpoint users and 300 servers. He has set up Meaningbit with two partners, which aims to improve working lives by using psychology and technology. He started by going on a national speaking tour *Bots, Burnout and Blame: Using technology to build better organisations*. He sounds as though he's having a ball being idealistic and learning a lot as well. Free of a day job, he seems to have seen a light, a need and a mission.

Will Arnold-Baker, aged 48, gave up a big job as MD of the advertising organization, Publicis UK. He'd been there 13 years holding together some important revenue-earning accounts like Army Recruitment and Morrisons supermarkets. The 'let's do it ourselves now' moment in founding the advertising agency, Come the Glorious Day, with two creatives, Matt and Steve, was, he says, no big deal, just obvious and overdue. They bootstrapped the business. He says in working for a big company he was surrounded by 'oxygen eaters'. He loves the speed of decision making and the fearless candour of the conversations the partners have now. His is the story of a mature start-up engineer pulling all the levers for success and exuding confidence and optimism. He says, 'not many people know how to make money in business'. We suspect he's an exception.

John Osborne was MD of a division of the Conviviality Group. The total group went into administration in 2018 as he stood aghast and watched from his division. He's now, phoenix-like, setting up a new wine distribution business. He has set a series of lessons, values and rules for his business: gain trust, get the values clear and written in granite, 'stick to basics, focus, don't try too many things, be patient and – always – be clear that people are the first and key focus'. He wants to build a business not just go on a race for growth as Conviviality had done.

Mentors, experts and dreamers

Laurence Collins, an ex Deloitte partner, is a mentor fulfilling a dream: helping young start-ups get it right, using his experience and contacts to be a one-man incubator.

Russell Bragg keeps on creating new businesses. He was badly burnt in a previous partnership but has risen again with a series of global hotel and residential developments on which he's advising.

Mike Kirsch has a long successful career in the financial sector as a director of financial services firm Aviva, and CEO of a series of financial companies and building societies he's helped turn around. He's also always dreamt of owning his own fishery. Cherry Lakes is the name and it's become a profitable, growing, respected business, not merely a hobby.

Peter Lederer is ex-Chairman of Gleneagles, ex-Director of Diageo Scotland, ex-Chairman of Visit Scotland and was awarded the CBE for his services to the hospitality sector. He's now a serial chairman and NED of three big Scottish businesses including Baxter's Soup, and the companies he's helping include three start-ups: Applecrate, Pod Global Solutions and Taste Communication. He knows more about customer service than almost anyone we know.

What's their driving motive?

All the serious 'give up my job to start again' people knew it was time to break free and have worked hard at getting all the details and the basic processes right. It was time to do it because they knew that they had to create their own 'thing'. It was a now-or-never moment. Money was secondary to the thrill of creation for all of them. John Eustace as an observer of the motivations of his Portuguese tech start-ups is impressed by their brightness and enthusiasm but cynical about their constant dreams of easy, massive wealth. What our group of seasoned entrepreneurs all share is an unromantic love of business and a pragmatic view of risk and reward.

What's it been like?

Overall, it's been smoother than might have been expected. Spence and Arnold-Baker realize they should have done it earlier, but Spence has found the transition from the comfort of a senior executive to the penury of a start-up a little trying. What stands out overall is the sense of achievement and job satisfaction. There was hardly any of the whingeing that is characteristic of interviews with people working for big corporations.

What's gone right?

The biggest thing that went right for Matthew Bellringer was going on a programme called *The Happy Start-Up* School that describes itself as the antidote to business as usual and has people talking about stuff like 'inclusivity, fear-fighting, and how to keep moving forward when you're too "in your head"'.

Another thing that went right is a tribute to vision and investment over caution. When Mike Kirsch created the best Fishing Lakes in Somerset with super luxury lodges, he discovered it was a bigger and more expensive project than he'd anticipated. But, as the project developed, he turned it into working like a proper business not the hobby that he started. By the middle of 2018, after five years of trading, 5,000 people had stayed at the site; he employs a full-time manager, three cleaners and he and his wife have a nice lakeside house. So, it's a decent business in its own right, as well as a dream made real. And it's growing. He's just acquired two more lakes.

What's gone wrong?

Nothing. Maybe they just forgot the bad moments. Russell Bragg reflected on the truth about business with this quote from Tim Fargo, angel investor and entrepreneur:

> Success is normally found in a pile of mistakes...mistakes should be examined, learned from, and discarded; not dwelled upon and stored.

Biggest disappointments

There were three disappointments that came up in many conversations:

- The first months or year can be tougher than expected.
- The first flush of success and being busy delivering an order or a service can make you forget that you've got to keep filling the pipeline.
- You've got to learn to spend valuable time with people. It takes more time than anyone expects.

Biggest (useful) learnings

- Promises take longer to come true than we can imagine. This is because potential customers are so busy that our project stays in their 'in-tray' for longer than we'd hoped.
- Working hard at the relationships in our own business so they don't deteriorate through either side having unrealistic expectations is essential. Truth isn't desirable; it's key to answering the basic question, 'what precisely do *we want* out of this joint adventure?'

The four real start-ups all look promising as good, solid, cash-generative businesses. None of them is burningly ambitious, being much more concerned to do it well than become huge. But then again, that's how Abbott Mead Vickers started, small but focused on quality. All the rest have modest ambitions but all can afford to relax a little and encourage their business to mature at its own pace. None is being tyrannized by the need for fast exits (apart from those tech businesses under John Eustace's wing). John himself is still driven by the idea of money rather than the need to spend it, that and a voracious sense of competitiveness. Mike Kirsch has become a 'lake magnate' because he can't help it and because he has an adhesive relationship with success.

A more global perspective

Asia-Pacific

Any visit to China provides jaw-dropping evidence of huge growth and a sense of confident enterprise. Billion dollar businesses are relatively commonplace, but it isn't just these unicorns that impress, it's the overall opportunistic attitude that's striking. Evan Osnos, in his 2015 book *Age of Ambition: Chasing fortune, truth and faith in the new China,* describes the fever that is created by anything new and exciting. Imagine, he says, the Industrial Revolution in the UK, only 100 times bigger and 10 times faster.

To get another perspective, cross to Korea where the global pop scene is being transformed by the creation of K-Pop groups. In August 2018 *Love Yourself: Answer* went to No. 1 in the US charts and *Idol* overwhelmed Taylor Swift in terms of online views. Even in London, their O2 Arena shows sold out in minutes. They mostly sing in Korean, they are scrubbed clean, are wholesome, have surgically enhanced faces and are 100 per cent perfectly in harmony and dance step. They could almost be human clones. This is a huge industry where each group is a start-up. At the last count there were 191 of them – an example of how start-ups are launched impressively market-ready in Asia.

Meanwhile in India there's a start-up boom. The wealthy of Mumbai apparently regard saying, 'I'm funding this start-up', as a smart conversational gambit at dinner parties (a new concept – a start-up as a pet). Nikunj Sha is an investor in new businesses. He has big family wealth backing him and says funding is no longer the problem: 'people are scrambling to get money away... an email request for funding can (often) have the round closed in minutes'.

Critically, the quality of new start-ups is excellent – the best IT graduates and the smartest young people are turning their backs on the old economy and going it alone, or in partnership in a start-up. In an economy growing at 7½ per cent and predicted (by some) to be heading to 9 per cent growth, the entrepreneurial boom seems unstoppable. Bureaucracy, says Deepak Vasandri, himself an entrepreneur, is a lessening problem but still a costly and time-consuming burden. He says the key skill differentiating an entrepreneur is *jugaad,* a Hindi term meaning hustler; a person with a can-do attitude; someone who thinks on their feet, who has an innovative, low-cost solution to a problem. If we publish in Hindi this book should be titled *Jugaad* – it's such a great word.

Australia, although a small market, has always been a centre for innovation. Donna Oakley-Davies is British but has lived and worked in Australia for many years. She's worked for Heinz, Kellogg's, SC Johnson and is now Marketing and Category Director of US $1 billion Primo Small Goods, and says of Australian business culture, 'I believe Australians are some of the most entrepreneurial people in the world'. She identifies two key trends matched in all other markets:

- The younger 18- to 30-year-olds who have seen what their parents have sacrificed and, in consequence, are doing their own thing.
- The middle-aged who are disillusioned with corporate life.

The United States: where the next new thing is another unicorn

We sometimes underestimate the biggest economy in the world and take it for granted. Get in a cab at Kennedy Airport and as you approach the city of New York, just look at that skyline and we'll defy you not to feel a rush of excitement. In the 1980s, when the Royal Bank of Scotland and WPP had become players on Wall Street and Madison Avenue, people like us felt we'd been accepted into an exclusive club on a more or less equal basis. We kept on pinching ourselves, hardly believing it was true. And, of course, it wasn't in the long run.

The United States is very different: it's landmass is over 100 times bigger than the UK and its GDP is seven times ours. But the biggest difference of all is their can-do attitude; a mindset that constantly seeks opportunities, shakes them, kicks those in the way and vigorously goes for it or, like a dog, trots onto the next entrepreneurial lamp post.

The United States is brilliant at casting. Thus, at the University of Pennsylvania, the university, together with Johnson & Johnson, has created 'Pennovation', a centre of entrepreneurial excellence and innovation in medicine. Elliott Curzon, a respected veteran in marketing and communication, says he's blown away by the work being done and how it gives new meaning to the word 'breakthrough'.

Moving onto the next new thing is the way things work here. Here, people pivot with an ease that Europeans can't. Steve Cranford from the Midwest trains as a lawyer, becomes a prosecuting attorney; pivots to become a senior executive at Rent-A-Centre, a furniture and electronics rent-to-own company; sells it, sells it well and realizes he loves the process of selling, using words to change the world; so he sets up an ad agency in LA; then realizing New York's where the epicentre of advertising really is , closes in LA and sets up in the Big Apple. Steve is not just an entrepreneurial pivoter; he's an ice skater doing the quadruple axel (no one's ever done a quadruple, but if Steve were a skater he probably would). Only in the United States.

Africa: the new future

Africa is very, very big and looking at the Mercator map is misleading. Few realize that the African landmass is bigger than the United States, China, India and most of Europe combined. And apart from being one of the richest in terms of mineral resources, Africa has a rapidly expanding population. By 2050 around 20 per cent of the world's people – some 2½ billion people – will be African. Already today with a median age of 20 compared to the world median of 40, Africa is stamping its demographic significance.

There are big challenges, but communication and a mobile banking infrastructure are not amongst them (mobile ownership is 93 per cent, about the same as the UK). And if you think that this is a male-focused continent, think again. In 11 countries – that's 20 per cent of Africa – women hold around a third of the seats in their respective parliaments.

Magatte Wade, who appeared earlier, diagnoses the core problem of lack of business activity leading to the emigration crisis. Why are people leaving Africa? She asks:

Why? Because they have no money.

Why? Because there are no jobs.

Why? Because there are no businesses.

Why? Because it's too difficult to set them up – what with stupid laws, taxes, tariffs – it's like swimming through molasses.

Dr Lesley Corbin, who runs a thriving consultancy in organizational psychology and leadership in the UK, educated herself out of Apartheid South Africa by hard work and effort of will. She won a Fulbright Scholarship to Columbia University, New York. She's a role model of endeavour and a tribute to the benefits of learning. Two women, two solutions to entrenched problems. Determination and autodidactic passion.

Africa may be the new future, but there's a mountain to climb mostly by overcoming old-fashioned thinking, bureaucracy and politics. China is pledging a further US $60 billion of infrastructure development funding for the three-year period up to 2021 on top of the billions already funded. But the sums required to modernize Africa's infrastructure to targets set by the UN amount to trillions not billions.

Europe: the biggest ever economic union of diverse countries

At US $16 trillion (excluding the UK), the EU is the second biggest economy in the world with some of the most famous global brands from Chanel to BMW to Gucci to Lego. More specifically, Europe has muscled a marketing story from its history to create the biggest array of luxury brands in the world. But growth rates of the collective economy are historically low. The EU Entrepreneurship 2020 Action Plan shows that apparently only 37 per cent of Europeans want to be self-employed compared with more than 50 per cent in the United States and China.

Recent research in the UK shows, amongst the young, as many as 70 per cent would like to be self-employed, so there seems to be a wide but understandable gap. Europeans have traditionally been more prone to espouse safe, secure careers in banks, public service and large businesses like BASF, Renault, Tetra Pak, AXA, VW, Fiat and BNP Paribas. They tend to be more obedient employees, certainly more obedient than the British. Think about the Netherlands, Sweden, Finland, Denmark, Greece, Portugal and you don't think so much of work–life balance as life–work balance. The most popular painting in Denmark is *Hip, hip hurrah*. It's cheers for the good life there.

However, there are exceptions. In Spain, for instance, young talent expresses itself in people like 26-year-old Raphael Ferrer Sánchez, the Zaragoza entrepreneur. When we spoke, he was having an *al fresco* family lunch in the autumn sun at his parents' home in a hill village near Zaragoza before going back to the office. He was one of the brightest, most composed, civilized and balanced young people we talked to anywhere in the world.

In Italy, Naples has generally been seen as *squilibrato* – a lovely word that's so expressive meaning 'unbalanced'. Typified by an epidemic of petty crime like handbag snatching, endemic poverty and a brooding Mafia presence, Naples had 50 per cent unemployment amongst the young. It had, but it has no more.

The tide has turned with the arrival of the Apple Developer Academy, based at the University Frederico II. The Academy takes 400 students a year from 25 countries (since opening in 2016 it's taken in 1,000 students). Cisco and Deloitte Digital have followed Apple to Naples and now, after Milan, Naples is the biggest region for young start-ups in Italy. Neapolis means new city. It shows what can be done by a kick-start like that provided by Apple's vote of confidence.

Portugal was one of the most tragic casualties in the 2008 financial crash. Now it's clawed itself back from the brink due in part to the government's vote of confidence in innovation. It has set aside €0.5 billion for start-ups in the areas of tech, life sciences and tourism and is the most active venture capital operation in Portugal. John Eustace, who's been hired to mentor its members, manage the fund and help it succeed, is impressed by the ingenuity and enthusiasm of the young tech geniuses. But this is a tough world in which high tech, if seen as promising, is stolen by global developers. There is not much honour around in business nowadays. But what there is, as John acknowledges, is an abundance of young brilliance and idealism.

In Poland, GDP is growing annually at 4.6 per cent and the Poles, to no one's surprise, are working incredibly hard and optimistically given the strong entrepreneurial climate. There were around 2,400 start-ups in 2015, over half of which were self-funding. Because Poland is the second largest ICT market in Central and Eastern Europe, it attracts more players into the sector. There are now an estimated 500,000 enterprises and 17,000 Polish ICT experts. Having Samsung set up a big R&D centre has acted like the magnet of Apple in Naples. The general view is that Poland is on the verge of breakthrough. Start-ups in Poland up to now have been mostly founded by relatively experienced business people, a third of whom are women. However, Poland is still considered a bit cumbersome in terms of bureaucracy. But what many see in the typical start-ups – determination, hard work and creativity – make Poland one of the places most likely to win the 'Euro-War of Enterprise'.

Going well: more to do

Continental Europe is more conservative and less disruptive in terms of entrepreneurial activity. There are some good stories and one of them, the Naples revival, is the most impressive and unusual. However, it's in Asia, the United States and the UK that the more radical and enterprising activity is found. We suspect the Euro-millennials will help change the landscape as they're beginning to do in the Iberian Peninsula.

Start-ups: lessons, surprises and insights – a summary

Are we now persuaded to throw off the shackles and set up Bell Hall Limited? The answer, somewhat to our surprise, because the frisson of excitement in a start-up is so intoxicating, is that's appealing. Yet we'd prefer to, more usefully, mentor new businesses harnessing their creative energies.

In a world so uncertain politically, socially, culturally and economically, being in control of our own destiny strikes deep chords into our collective soul.

There are a few surprises in our research. Generally, there has been less ambition to get rich than might have been expected. Higher motives to 'change the world' are less mentioned than the deep need to create great, little businesses. The sense that doing this is a worthwhile legacy to aim for, rather than having a salaried career, was widespread.

In a world so uncertain politically, socially, culturally and economically, being in control of our own destiny strikes deep chords into our collective soul. We have talked to many people in

IT, catering or automotive repairs who are happy doing what they love whilst earning relatively small and erratically produced sums of money. Not everyone is immune to money – enjoying spending it or needing to have it – but the profit motive is a factor reducing in relevance. There's another factor mentioned by several. This is the ability to earn money by freelancing whilst starting up a no- or low-earning business. Insofar as we can stereotype them, start-ups are a mix of visionaries, idealists and pragmatists. And, of course, that remote possibility of surprising wealth is not completely out of the question.

Our three cohorts on whom we've focused – millennials, women and ex-executives – have different motives and ways of going about things, but they are unified in their desire to create a legacy and to do what they do very well. Only one or two of our quite large sample would settle for cash in return for creating a so-so business. Millennials and women, we discovered, are jointly changing the management styles and priorities in new businesses. They're making the world of work a better place. Theirs is a kinder, more collaborative and creative place in which to live.

No one pretends starting a new business is easy or devoid of big challenges, but, as opposed to the ritual of office routine, people find making it up as they go along is a bit scary but very inspiring and exciting.

Of all the advice that we have to give, or have got from others, there are five key things that stand out:

1 Don't be alone. Have partners, advisers and other start-ups to talk to.
2 Value yourself and your values.
3 Rigorously plan how to operate a smooth-running business (this is not a hobby).
4 Get a mentor with energy, experience and a sense of humour.
5 Enjoy the challenge…feel that buzz…celebrate the 'wins'.

There is a start-up revolution happening. If we want to be part of it, we'll find ourselves in good company. If we have a clear set of values and resilience, what happens can surprise us. David Abbott, co-founder of Abbott Mead Vickers, made this astute observation to the Chair of their lawyers, Roger Alexander: 'no one expected us to get this big by just trying to be better'.

CHAPTER THREE

Pivots, refinements and surprises

What is a pivot?

The word 'pivot' entered the business lexicon briefly in 2011 thanks to Eric Ries, US entrepreneur and blogger. He wrote a seminal book *The Lean Startup* in which he defined 'pivoting' more clearly: 'We keep one foot rooted in what we've learnt so far whilst making a fundamental change in strategy'. Eric's point though is a good one. A 'pivot' is not a radical rethink, it's a shift in strategic direction. The way we see it, a 'pivot' is rather like 'tacking' in sailing, using the wind created by customer input to find the way to achieve the most productive momentum.

And what has ever been the point in being intransigent in the face of evidence that your original thinking might not be correct? Master economist John Maynard Keynes was clear about what was required in such circumstances: 'When events change I change my mind. What do you do?'

That we should have to debate this point is illustrative of the often malevolent power that some unimaginative investors in business can have. Like politicians they don't like the word *sorry* so, when Larry Kim CEO of Mobile Monkey said in 2019, 'a pivot is a glorified way of saying "oops"', we can see how pivoting might cause some people problems.

However, the real world in which we live is in so constant a state of flux or revolution that a 'pivot' should not be a cause for embarrassment. Instead, it's a key strategic tool. This fluctuating world calls for a number of qualities from the start-up manager. They must be resilient and implacably good humoured in the face of setbacks; they must retain their open mindedness and creative joy in life; they must be agile and nimble-minded. Above all, they must be able and happy to pivot. Pivot is not a euphemism for cock-up or failure.

Lisa Matthews, whom we've profiled elsewhere in *Start-ups, Pivots and Pop-ups*, has been very clear about the role and importance of the flexibility that pivoting allows: 'The big word for any start-up is "pivot". If the evidence says something is wrong change it...in other words, PIVOT'.

A brief history of pivots

Jack Welch's reinvention of GE in the 1980s was a classic exercise in pivoting. When he became CEO, he inherited a vast sprawling empire of a company. It was a huge business that was making decent profits, but it was fat, complacent and its very congeniality was a sticky impediment to taking hard decisions. The pivot was to shift the ambition towards making every part of the business number one or two in its sector. Amongst Welch's engaging, handwritten notes he has one that says: 'Fix, Sell or Close'. In the early years GE sold 71 businesses, which generated US $0.5 billion and completed 118 other deals that cost US $1 billion. He was called 'Neutron Jack' because of the incredibly forthright approach and the merciless killing of sacred cows. GE was a good company, but with the impact of his strategic shift it became a great company. 'Fix, Sell or Close' was one of the most potent, pivotal statements any conglomerate has made.

The Saatchi brothers' redefinition of what advertising was and did in the 1980s was critical to the subsequent success of British advertising. It too was built around a very simple statement: 'Anything is Possible'. This was a shamelessly hyperbolic statement and one that any brand owner wanted to believe, even if they knew it wasn't really quite true. The company developed a sense of unstoppable momentum, winning many of the iconic advertising accounts of the time, including British Airways, itself under the inspirational and pivotal leadership of Lord King and Colin Marshall. Their slogan 'The World's Favourite Airline' captured the swagger of patriotism that the early Thatcher years engendered in the 1980s business world. Saatchi's also created the advertising for the Conservative Party and, for a while, with the ebullient Tim Bell at the helm, it seemed almost as though they, Saatchi & Saatchi, were running the country. Well, as they themselves said, 'Anything is Possible'.

The story about pivoting that stands out in the 2000s, apart from the big Silicon Valley successes, is potentially as important. James Dyson has built a company that's transformed the world of household appliances. This seems at first sight too prosaic a feat to win a 'Pivotal Decoration'. But it's what this leads to that matters. He is developing battery systems that give long life and power. His real and next target is cracking the automotive battery challenge. Dyson is a classic inventor. Back in the 1970s he allegedly created the iconic toy, the Spacehopper, and the garden vehicle, the Ball Barrow. Now he is a global player with a £3.5 billion company, employing 12,000 people selling premium-priced, new generation appliances and is poised to be a player in the world of transport. The pivot story here is about his mastering mobile, clean, lightweight, long-lasting power.

Pivots that were less successful include Enron and Conviviality. All of these fell under the definition of setting big, hairy, audacious targets and claims of prospective riches, but they gambled not so much on the wrong horse as gambling on a horse that didn't actually exist.

These are all stories that are well documented. That of Conviviality – a failure of recent years – is about a pivot based on gambling on growth. Diana Hunter has been demonized for the group's collapse, but her eight-year career at Waitrose, creating 'Little Waitrose', demonstrated real skill and attention to detail. Sadly, between 2013 and 2018, she went from being CEO of Bargain Booze, a small chain of off-licences, to creating the Conviviality Empire, based on a breakneck acquisition trail reaching market capitalization of £0.75 billion in 2016. *The Buyer*, the on-trade magazine, said this, 'The new Conviviality business may now be the biggest drinks operator in the UK...the ball has been pushed off the mountain and it is only going to get bigger...Game on' (Siddle, 2019).

However, the chase for growth imploded and a series of profit warnings led briskly to the company's collapse. The irony of course is that all the accepted wisdom is that women will tend to adopt a more cautious, building-a-sustainable-business-with-sound-foundations approach. Diana Hunter saw things differently and so, of course, did her backers. It's still tough times for booze. Oddbins collapsed in early 2019 and it probably won't stop there.

Enron is beyond description. Somewhere between *Game of Thrones*, the *Sopranos* and *Mission Impossible*, Enron sits as an example of disproving the claim that anything's possible. It isn't. Enron was a US energy, commodities and services company based in Houston, Texas. It was founded in 1985, ultimately employed 29,000 staff and had claimed revenues of nearly US $101 billion during 2000. *Fortune* named Enron 'America's Most Innovative Company' for six consecutive years. In 2001 it filed for bankruptcy. Its revenues were shown to have been sustained by accounting fraud (BBC News Website, 2019). Its demise also caused the dissolution of the Arthur Andersen accounting firm, Enron's main auditor for years. Yet it wasn't quite as simple as bare-faced fraud. What Enron did was disclose everything it did, concealing nothing. The trouble was no one understood what the business model depended on. First, Enron guessed future income from contracts and showed that as income averaged out over the life of the contract. Second, in order to raise capital, Enron set up SPEs (special purpose entities) at arm's length from the company, against which cheap money could be borrowed and then lent back to the company. No one seems to have understood all this, not Arthur Andersen, not the top people at Enron, not the media, not the regulators.

Except (and this is the most alarming aspect of the story) a lot of companies in corporate America at around this time were pivoting their businesses around similar versions of 'creative accounting'. But it was all there to see in the quarterly statements that companies have to produce in the United States (10Ks), which are incredibly long and comprehensive; too long usually for anyone to bother reading.

The other thing about Enron was it was actually trying to be an excellent company. The *Fortune* awards for innovation were not ironic, they were real. Enron was top of the league for attracting talent, helped by McKinsey, who kept close to Enron throughout. During the 1990s Enron was hiring 290 of the best MBAs each and every year. The company employed very smart minds. These were not thugs, crooks or stupid. Enron's one-time CEO Kenneth Lay said, 'we hire very smart people and we pay them more than they think they are worth'. These smart minds were being hired to think outside the box. By the way, if we believe that everyone needs to think outside the box, maybe it's the box that needs fixing (as Malcolm Gladwell observed in his book of 2009, *What the Dog Saw*).

The lessons from Enron are that being creative, clever and original in the interpretation of numbers is possibly foolish and certainly dangerous. And even more important is the fact that we daren't hire or rely on just very clever people who create things no one else understands. We need to hire smart, honest and pragmatic people who ask lots of questions and talk in simple terms.

For some, pivot stands for high risk. For others, it's a prudent strategic adjustment. For some, a pivot can seem like a step out of the window in a tall skyscraper. But, obviously, it's not good enough to pivot if that means scrapping all the good stuff too. Go back to the wise Eric Ries's comment, 'We keep one foot rooted in what we've learnt so far whilst making a fundamental change in strategy'.

How pivoting works in practice now

Start-ups depend on making decisions about what risks to take

We know a lot about many things. We can send a probe 4 billion miles into outer space and film a dark, icy rock we've called Ultima Thule, or we can send the Parker Solar Probe into space, ultimately to touch the sun, but we are still at sea when it comes to understanding the human brain and how it behaves in facing decisions.

The most useful work on this mystery is to be found in Daniel Kahneman's 2012 book *Thinking, Fast and Slow*. In it there are a series of theses that are very relevant to the start-up and the way they make (or fail to make) decisions. Here are a few of the most relevant. They are, necessarily, rather cryptically explained compared with Daniel's more eloquent prose.

Availability – where data shows people are highly influenced by easy-to-remember and recent, anecdotal evidence: 'My wife thinks…'; 'I heard someone say …'. The influence of social media rather than hard data has exacerbated this tendency to regard 'available' evidence as significant.

Loss aversion – people are more determined to prevent losing what they have than make a perfectly reasonable decision to risk going for gain – the classic entrepreneur shows less evidence of being risk averse than this.

Optimistic bias – this is one of the most dangerous traits. In planning anything, people tend consistently to overestimate sales and underestimate costs. On a more day-to-day basis, research showed in planning kitchen refurbishments the costs were on average underestimated by buyers by almost 50 per cent.

Sunk costs – the propensity to put good money after bad, as opposed to cutting our losses and pivoting to a new solution, is prevalent. Deep down, people want to avoid the failure of wasting money and fail to see the irony that spending more money on a lost cause will usually only make things worse.

Overconfidence – we think we are more in control of our environment and lives than is in fact the case. External factors such as what competitors are doing, or simply luck, can have a much greater impact than our own skill and power.

All the evidence, Kahneman tells us, suggests we are more influenced by our emotions than our rational thinking. However hard we may try to be rational there are intuitive biases tugging away at the decision-making levers in our brain, making us do what we feel like doing, not what we think is the rationally right thing to do. Men are especially prone to this, many believing that their decision is the result of a deeply rational conclusion and an example of alpha male leadership, getting to the heart of the issue rather than being the product of emotion, prejudice and bias. Watch male politicians debating anywhere in the world and see this tendency illustrated in strident colour.

Reid Hoffman made billions in founding LinkedIn and has enough success behind him to make what he says worth listening to. In an interview with CNBC by Adam Bryant, CEO of Merryck & Company, the mentoring and leadership business and ex-journalist for the *New York Times* in December 2018, Hoffman is very clear that, 'if your confidence falls...pivot... you're always learning and adjusting'.

He speaks animatedly, almost evangelically, about the need to spread entrepreneurial fervour around the world. We love his definition of the entrepreneurial sweet spot as *healthy craziness*.

He admires big, bold decisions because these usually go behind a simple, focused idea. LinkedIn, for instance, started as a job recruitment concept addressing employers who had jobs to fill. Quickly it became an employee site on which you planted your CV for all to see, and then simply *the* business people's network site that, in turn, became a hugely valuable recruitment/job-seeking site and the must-use site even for those in business and even for those who avoid social media. It has 590 million members in 200 countries.

Reid acknowledges the tension that exists between persistence and flexibility in start-ups but thinks the two can co-exist so long as business owners continue to peer deeply into every aspect of their consumers' behaviour. In the end, it's the way that people feel, think and behave that determines a business success, not how clever its algorithm is. Reid doesn't just use the words *scale-up*, he uses *blitz scale*, which expresses the urgency of his growth ambition and the dynamic of his thinking. Only in the United States (and possibly China now) could this happen. Others in the United States – Steve Cranford, Zach Rosner and Elliott Curzon – are aligned in thinking that it's our ability to keep on learning and our life's experience that aids innovation and informs a strategic pivot.

The difference between the US blitz scale in the 'big, hairy, audacious goal' world of business (that's a term coined by US authors and organizational consultants Jim Collins and James Porras in 1994 in their book *Built to Last*) and the more circumspect European business world is captured in this story about sport. One of the UK's sporting heroes, Robin Cousins the ice skater, Olympic Champion, European Champion and three times world champion in the 1980s, went to the United States for some top-up coaching. Allegedly he was told he had a problem because he

It's only when you fall or fail that you know what your limits are and how far you have to go to win.

didn't skate to fall. It's only when you fall or fail that you know what your limits are and how far you have to go to win. Americans generally skate to fall.

In the 2018 Nike advertisement featuring the star Quarterback American Football Player Colin Kaepernick (who ceased playing because he 'gave the knee' to the US National Anthem and was banned from his sport) uses this to make his point: 'Don't ask if your dreams are crazy. Ask if they're crazy enough'.

That is pivot talk. Don't stay in your comfort zone. Don't just persevere. Skate to fall. Think healthily crazy.

Often the risks of starting a new business are greater if you hang back and try to play safe. Maybe you aren't quite in the hairy audacity mindset yet, but you need ambition and energy. Risks are part of our everyday lives and should be thrilling not paralysing unless you're content to be like US journalist and humourist Robert Benchley who wrote in jest, 'Sometimes I'm so worried about what might happen that I stay in bed. There I worry about falling out and breaking something'.

Atula Abeysekera, Senior Risk Officer at Schroders, the UK multinational asset management company, started life as an engineer and sees risk as relating to common sense and to the soundness of a plan's foundations:

> Starting your own business is risky. Half of all new businesses fail
> in the first five years. But whatever the risk involved the task is
> to manage risk...not avoid it. At sea the wind can propel you or
> capsize you. Sail *with* that wind of risk and use it.

Risk then is a management issue not a gambling issue or indeed an issue to be avoided. It's as simple as this: think about how to benefit from taking risks, not about avoiding them.

How to pivot to good effect

We've already had good advice. We mustn't let our confidence ebb away because our current approach isn't working. We must make sure we're working with hard evidence plus intuition but not with intuition alone. The most important evidence will be what our customers say to us. But beware, because although they may not realize it themselves, they don't always tell the truth. Remember what David Ogilvy said about research: 'People don't think what they feel, don't say what they think and don't do what they say'.

It's not that human beings are habitual liars; it's just that sometimes they say what they think we want to hear and sometimes they don't know what they think but don't want to seem stupid, so they just say what comes into their head. It takes greater intelligence than most of us have to realize that 'I don't know' is often the right and the best answer.

It takes greater intelligence than most of us have to realize that 'I don't know' is often the right and the best answer.

Equally, changing our mind proves that we're still thinking. Being dogmatic isn't a sign of strength, it's a sign of stubbornness. Pivoting, as we've said, should be seen as a natural thing to do not a guilty admission of being wrong. Which is not to decry perseverance and resilience so long as we don't fall victim to what is called *design fixation* – a love affair with our baby of an idea that blinds us to the truth so that we'll hear nothing ill of it. They also call this a 'maladaptive defence mechanism', which is a posh way of describing a condition more popularly called *cloth ears*.

It's important we squash the notion that pivoting is a sign of failure. The contemporary notion many people have, that failure is just great, can be rather silly ('I crashed the car when making a call on my mobile – great learning…life enriching'). Elon Musk (Mr Tesla) put it like this:

> Failure is an option here. If things are not failing you are not innovating enough. (Satara, 2019)

Clearly Elon is a genius, but equally clearly, he's a bit eccentric. This celebrating failure thing is distinctly weird. Whilst pivoting or changing direction and trying hard to explore the limits of what can be done can be admirable, constant failure is less so. A pivot is a planned alteration; failure is a cock-up. Our final point on this is that the adjective for 'fail' is 'failed'; the adjective for 'pivot' is 'pivotal'. According to the *Oxford Dictionary*, pivotal means 'being of crucial importance in relation to the development or success of something'. And that sounds rather good; certainly much better than 'failed'.

The reasons for pivoting are variously when:

- Our customers tell us our proposition or product is not for them.
- Our financial advisers tell us the business model doesn't and won't make any money.
- Since deciding on our business model, things in the market have changed.
- A competitor comes out with a better (and possibly cheaper) product.
- We find our business increasingly personally uninspiring.

The last phenomenon was suffered by Casey Schorr of Print-fection, a Denver, Colorado-based company, formed in 2006, that helps businesses market themselves with promotional merchandise. He said, 'I didn't want to spend years working on something I wasn't passionate about. I knew we needed to pivot'. So, in 2011, he persuaded his team to pivot from being an on-demand t-shirt printing fulfilment service company to being a business-to-business marketing consultancy, shifting the way companies think about and use branded promotional swag (which is, incidentally, also called *schwag*, *tchotchkes* or *freebies* in the United States).

Example of a foundering start-up and how a pivot saved the day

Place: Zaragoza, Spain.

Founder: Raphael Ferrer Sánchez, aged 22 at the time of the pivot.

Background: Computer Studies degree at Zaragoza – thinking about a start-up on graduating.

Start-up idea: A bracelet children wear that enables parents to track where they are.

Prize winner: A national prize for innovation.

Research: Gets a brilliant response – parents said they loved the idea.

Market test: But hardly anyone bought it.

Breakthrough thinking: When one parent said, 'no…don't really see the need for our kids but it would be great for my grandad…we need it to find him when he wanders off'.

Pivot: Position it (a necklace, bracelet or watch) for the elderly…a bigger market and a growing problem.

Result: Great success – seven employees currently – about to launch in Portugal and Italy (South America next).

Company: Neki.

Spanish proverb: 'A *wise* man changes his mind, a fool never.'

If we regard a pivot as a strategic tool and persuade investors, stakeholders and the media that it is just that – a navigational correction or a refinement based on intensive research with potential users, then all will be well. As it was with Raphael.

Investors in business are rigidly focused on their ROI and, given the failure rate, especially in the tech space, who can really blame them? But three things are useful to learn:

- Don't overuse pivots as a strategic tool. Constant pivoting will sap your energy, your investors' confidence and your funds. As Jeremy Bullmore, one-time Advisory Board Member of WPP, the advertising and marketing services conglomerate, allegedly once said: 'you can only turn the other cheek once'.

- Simplicity. We live in a world of jargon and complexity, and this is not good for our skills at communicating. Investors such as Warren Buffett demand simplicity. As so often he puts it pungently like this: 'You only want to invest in a business an idiot could run because one day an idiot will run it' (Holodny, 2019).
- Play each ball as it comes. Edward Johnstone started a business called the Sussex Peasant, a fresh food mobile business that only sells Sussex grown, produced and reared in Sussex food – we'll see more on him in the pop-up chapter of *Start-ups, Pivots and Pop-ups*. His wisdom is simple. Things go wrong in business. When they do, sort them out and work out how to stop them happening again.

The things that most often damage a start-up are a poor process and business system; a market that is less profitable, easy to reach or sizeable than we'd first thought; and, finally, having too little money. But the good news is we have this strategic tool called a 'pivot', which, when push comes to shove, can get us out of trouble if used well.

Pivoting and people

Increasingly, and especially in an increasingly automated world, a world of artificial intelligence and robots, it's people who still make the difference in business. Jack Welch's least astute assertion was about the potential for improving customer service by removing the human interface. In his 2003 book *Jack* he qualifies this obliquely by saying, 'In manufacturing we try to stamp out variance. With people, variance is everything'.

Bill's: a family business becomes a nationwide treasure

It's variance that leads to differentiation that leads to product and brand distinction and appeal. Which leads to the story of Bill's, the café/restaurant chain, and about four pivots.

Bill's started as a greengrocers in Lewes. Some customers said it was a bit expensive, but they also said it was rather good. Founder, Bill Collison, has always felt close to the soil and vegetables. He's a less posh Hugh Fearnley-Whittingstall, the celebrity River Cottage chef. All was going well at Bill's the family greengrocers until 2000. Then Lewes flooded and their shop was wrecked.

THE FIRST PIVOT: 'GROWING UP'

Bill was so depressed he apparently wanted to close down, but the family persuaded him to re-open the shop together with an addition – a café mostly using fresh vegetables as the key ingredient. It was a great success. It's an interesting lesson that it took a disaster to cut through the inertia or sheer conservatism and inject some innovation into the business concept.

THE SECOND PIVOT: 'HAVING ONE BABY'

In 2005 Bill's Brighton opened with the same formula, but now it was much more café with fewer vegetables. Brighton was regarded as a big leap at the time because there was a lot more competition there, albeit a much bigger footfall than in Lewes. There was a question many visitors to Brighton asked: 'Why there couldn't be a Bill's where they lived?' So why wasn't Bill's franchised throughout the UK? It was obvious that the family who owned the company had neither the stomach nor the money for such an expensive and complex adventure. What was obvious to anyone, not least the 11 million visitors to Brighton every year, was that Bill's was special. Great home cooking. Great value. Great opportunity.

THE THIRD PIVOT: 'SELLING AND SPREADING'

Richard Caring (investor in Soho House and owner of the Ivy, J. Sheekey, Caprice, Côte – now sold – Sexy Fish and Wentworth Golf Club) bought the two Bill's outlets in 2008. He was not particularly flattering about the outlets, saying they 'needed help'. Reinventing Bill's as a chain as opposed to two slightly quirky, south coast cafés needed a lot of investment, thought and faith. Caring said he thought the brand needed a bit of love as it had fallen behind, but, he conceded, it had potential.

THE FOURTH PIVOT: 'DEFINING THE BRAND AND SHAKING THINGS UP'

Caring is interesting. His recent remarkable success is founded on creating a series of brilliant process-driven, strongly branded and clearly positioned restaurant chains. Bill's, against the purist marketeer's odds, has much improved (ironically Lewes where it all started is now one of the least impressive of its outlets.) In the past few years there's been management upheaval at Bill's with two CEOs lasting less than a year each. But Bill Collison is still actively involved and in 2018 there were 102 outlets. Sales grew by 7 per cent to just under £120 million with EBITDA increasing slightly to over £13 million.

DISTILLING THE SOUL OF THE BRAND

The new management seems to have spent a lot of time searching for and distilling the soul of the brand – it's casual 'home-cookingness' – it's all-day brunchiness' – it's fresh 'vegetableness'. All of these are very much part of the *zeitgeist*. The vegetable shop may have gone but the whiff of fresh vegetables is still there. So too is that shabby chic that gives it that authentic feel. It doesn't try too hard. It is one of the most English of restaurant outlets. But we suspect the next pivot could be to embrace and become the patron of the growing momentum for healthy eating, vegetarianism and flexitarianism.

Career pivots: a major change in what you do

In a world where the teenager of today is likely to have up to 15 very different jobs in their lifetime, the concept of career is over. Gordon Marsden, current MP for Blackpool South, worries that we may be creating a horizontal system in which each new job is learnt at a basic level before the person moves on to something completely different, again at a basic level. The economic issue and challenge with this model is people won't generate any salary progression. In contrast the vertical model of becoming increasingly more skilled in a specific job leads to enhanced value and earning capacity.

The most interesting personal and career pivots occur in later life, at 45 onwards, when the pivot is motivated by passion, altruism or conviction. Like the executive who became a vicar in his late fifties and gave up a big job in university administration. A late but urgent calling, and the word 'calling' is especially relevant.

Lucy Kellaway had a 'calling' when she gave up the job of being a leading columnist for the *Financial Times* to become a maths teacher. She co-founded 'Now Teach' (https://nowteach. org.uk/), designed to get mature executives into teaching. She expected a response but not a big one, certainly not the 1,000+ who applied; neither did she expect so many in her local group to survive the gruelling training course. Over 85 per cent did. She says her big mistake was underestimating how much skill she needed to succeed in teaching because it's much more complicated than writing columns for a newspaper. Working with teenagers is wonderful, starting a new life is exciting and having so many stories to tell is good. But it's exhausting and schools are very hierarchical places. Does she regret it? Not at all, but she can only do it, in the way she believes the job deserves, by working just three days a week.

Katy Paul-Chowdhury was once a fast-talking consultant for Schaffer Consulting in Stamford, Connecticut. She is now in Toronto writing and wondering why it took her so long to do something she loves, is good at and is independent of the billable-hours pressure all consultants feel. She talks about reinventing ourselves, and indeed all the people in this age group who've pivoted agree it's a pivot towards sanity and away from competitive stress. She's had a fresh start and says she likes more things than she dislikes and feels in control of her life...and, what's more, her writing's getting better too.

Atula Abeysekera is the Senior Risk Officer at Schroders and Professor of Practice (Risk Management) at Imperial College London. He started life as an engineer but having graduated decided to pivot and go into finance – he had a 'calling' to be an expert in risk. Despite being married with a new baby, he persevered with exams and penury and here he is today loving what he does and combining his disciplines saying, for instance, 'in assessing financial risk imagine you are looking at a building... start with the plan then look at the foundations and the overall structure...is it sound...will it last and so on'.

The big pivot

Rachel Melsom: from studying spreadsheets to bedsheets

When she was a young intern Rachel Melsom worked for an advertising agency where she was regarded as very bright and rather serious. She was utterly reliable, diligent and probably thought the world of *Mad Men* advertising was a mixture of inebriated, irresponsible adolescence and overhyped creativity.

Time passed and she went off to become a Director of Marketing at CBS, a senior manager at Virgin Media and then became a partner at Brunswick, the country's leading corporate relations and critical issues business. They are the go-to place for the best advice when you don't know what to do or say.

It was 2002 and as she watched friends in the city making indecent sums of money, she thought, 'why can't I be indecent like that too...I'm just as smart as them'. And she was, so she started a company called Media Asset Consulting Limited, which focused on helping companies exploit and monetize their intellectual property assets (surprisingly a lot of businesses have no idea what hidden values they may own and that they blithely give away or ignore). She was a co-director of this for six years before selling the business. With the entrepreneurial bit between her teeth she then started Media Matrix, which created a successful US Gameshow, in partnership with Elizabeth Murdoch who eventually bought control of the business.

So there's Rachel the businesswoman, entrepreneur and alpha talent. And here's the 'big pivot'. Having originally read Genetics at University College London in her late teens, she has now decided, in her mid-30s, to become a doctor.

It took four hard years at St George's Hospital Medical School plus two years Foundation Training at Worthing Hospital to add on to her three years in Genetics at University College. She described how she and fellow (younger) medics gathered round the TV watching *House* starring the incomparable Hugh Laurie and trying to out-diagnose him. She is now a member of the Department of Medicine for the Elderly at Worthing Hospital, caring for acutely unwell elderly patients with multiple co-morbidities. In addition she's the Director for the UK and Europe of Tobacco Free Portfolios, which campaigns to deter investors giving their investment money to tobacco companies.

We really like this story. Like Lucy Kellaway, Rachel has made a career pivot that puts a huge chunk back into society. Rachel, after her work in media and start-ups, is now doing what she might have done 20 years ago but now, rounded and burnished by her experience of life, is probably doing it with more passion, empathy and purpose than she would have done at a younger age.

Our brain's the fastest form of transport

We've been struck by how many of the people we've talked to have done second degrees or have PhDs. We have Matthew Bellringer doing a degree in Psychology at the Open University, Daniel Ross an MBA at London Business School, Richard French doing a BA at the University of East Anglia (just to show he could); PhDs or MScs to Kit Carruthers, Lisa Matthews, Becky

Sage, Sharon Varney, Elisabeth Kelan, Zara Nanu, Hannah Philp and, of course, Dr Rachel Melsom.

Women have always tended to take education more seriously than men, but as Harry Maitland, the nascent rock star (whom we saw in the section on millennials), is showing us, being super bright doesn't necessarily mean you have to do a degree to prove you're smart. However, in general terms, a decent, well-exercised and receptive brain helps in outsmarting competitors in business.

The world is changing and we need to create a race of enterprising business people creating new things, changing stuff and employing people. Robots are going to be a permanent feature of our lives, but human ingenuity will always prevail. It's interesting and, perhaps reassuring, that whilst robots are getting better and better at games like chess and Go, they are utterly hopeless at Pick-Up-Sticks and Kerplunk.

Pivoting in action

The smell of new paint, the ringing of phones, the buzz as you win

No one can forget that strange feeling of walking into your new business and doing something specific that reflects your ownership, like tidying up the magazines or washing an abandoned coffee cup. The way you behave in your own business, or a start-up of which you are a part, is completely different from what you do in a big corporation, so much so that long-serving corporates can often find the small-minded intimacy of the three-person start-up office rather awkward.

It's the decision-making process that is most different in a start-up. It's faster, no one's looking over their shoulder; it's easy to change your mind ('I was thinking about what we agreed again and I think I might have got it wrong'), and it seems more impactful in the sense you decide and act at once... there isn't a tortuous delay between deciding something and it happening. One of the most interesting aspects of the freedom of a start-up is the fearless candour with which ideas are espoused or ditched.

There's a constant narrative being put about by the government and leading thinkers about the importance of building a robust SME business sector, but the relentless quest for scale and global fame had, until recently, side-lined this imperative and, with it, the nimbleness of thinking that small, new businesses have.

But we believe that times have changed.

The owners of small businesses are always sprinting instead of lumbering along like the behemoths do. Nimbleness is something Peter Lederer, Scottish business leader and entrepreneur, has strong views about. When he chaired Gleneagles Hotel, he encouraged a sense of smooth, but apparently effortless urgency, in the place. Bruce Crouch, ex Creative Director of ad agency Bartle Bogle Hegarty, puts it in characteristically graphic terms:

> I like working with start-ups...they want to cut through the crap because that's what they've escaped from.

Several people have told us that pivoting dominates their whole life in a start-up, that the very uncertainty and chaos of that world is exhilarating but requires a new kind of energetic, open-minded responsiveness. In a world without rules you have to make quick decisions and have rock solid values. Seth Godin, the acclaimed management guru and author, defines what we could call 'pivot-planning' when he suggests in his 2018 book, *This is Marketing*, that the real fun (and the most important thing) is to figure a back-up for whatever could go wrong .

We are looking at a world of architects, not bricklayers, where people are, more often than not, simply in love with their product.

We are looking at a world of architects, not bricklayers, where people are, more often than not, simply in love with their product. It's a world of speed, agility and resourcefulness. So let's find out more.

Five pivoters and their stories

Embracing change and dealing with complexity

Two tech stories, one fast-moving consumer goods and one service business. A pivoted start-up, an idea meeting an existing business and sudden magic occurring, a pivot from same-as/good-enough transforming to leading edge and a thwarted ambition leading to a potential rebirth.

BECKY SAGE: 'IF YOU AREN'T PIVOTING YOU AREN'T THINKING'
Becky, who's CEO of Interactive Scientific Limited, lives daily with contradiction, innovation and change. The company describes what it does very simply in saying they make the invisible, molecular world become visible. Science, or indeed any advanced academic subject at the leading edge, pivots because new discoveries are being continually made. Scientific Interactive started life as an Arts Council project dramatizing science through Virtual Reality primarily for educational purposes. It still has an Ed Tech aspect but is increasingly focused on the scale-up opportunities that business provides.

First of all, Becky. A degree in Physics from the University of Bristol, UK, followed by a PhD in Laser Ablation, Plasma, Mass Spectrometry, Thin Film Deposition (topics familiar to all of us I imagine?). She also spent a year at the Los Angeles, American Academy of Dramatic Arts in her late twenties. As an actress she has a long list of performances to her name. She's also a keen gymnast, winning the adult British Gymnastic Championship in 2017 and 2018. So Becky is an unusually high achiever and one of the things that occurs to us is the truth of the adage, 'if you want to get something done ask someone who's busy'. Becky probably gets more done because she does more and has so many different perspectives. A line from one of her blogs encapsulates her philosophy: 'transition is the process of change, the journey to something new or different, and that's exciting'.

The company's invention of the Nano Simbox is changing the face of Ed Tech and scientific research. It's taken five years to perfect, and they've needed the £12.5 million seed capital, so they can now create high-powered scientific simulations that inform, involve and enthral. She says the company in effect thinks in 3D (isn't that the world we live in now? Isn't it 2D thinking in a 3D world that's causing so many misunderstandings and blunders from classroom to boardroom?).

Scientific Interactive is a disruptive business because it takes people who're exposed to its technology to places they'd previously only conceived of on paper or in theory not in simulated reality. It can pivot people from the present to the future to the possible. Yet interestingly, the same management issues exist here to a greater or lesser extent as in a business making pork pies:

- The issue of being a woman as CEO.
- The issues of managing a partnership.
- The exhaustion of leadership.

Becky, with her portfolio of gymnastics, acting, blogs, award ceremonies, being, for instance, a finalist in the HSBC Forward Ladies awards and, again, a finalist in the WISE woman in science tech in 2017, is obviously likely to feel a little tired. When Oracle selected Scientific Interactive as one of the start-ups to put on their accelerator programme, exhilaration and exhaustion must have competed with each other in her mind.

JASON BARBER'S STORY: 'MILKING A NEW OPPORTUNITY'

Jason Barber is a West Dorset dairy farmer with a 250-strong dairy herd. The thing he's proudest of is actually surviving in what is, in the UK, a beleaguered industry. His farm, which Jason took over from his father in 2000, is Seaborough Manor near Beaminster. The Barber family has been noted for great cheese for 200 years. In fact they won the World Cheese Awards Cheddar trophy in 2012. Jason's cousins, Chris and Giles Barber, are the cheese geniuses, while Jason has other ideas as to what he can do with milk by-products – specifically whey. He decided to make ... vodka.

Jason invented Black Cow Vodka after learning about the Tuva, a nomadic Siberian tribe, who for many centuries have been distilling Araka vodka made from fermented mares' milk. He wanted a new challenge, he really wanted a pivot, a new income stream, and this sounded exciting and a challenge. It took him some time to get it right, as the first vodkas he produced were, he confesses, frankly revolting. He makes the vodka by separating the curds (that's what makes his cheese) and whey (that he describes as the 'problem-child' of dairy). The whey is fermented into a beer; then, using a special yeast, the milk sugar is converted into alcohol. This 'milk beer' is then distilled, blended, triple filtered, finished and hand bottled. Every batch makes around 3,000 bottles. Black Cow is the world's first *pure* milk vodka. It was launched in May 2012 and in 2015 won Gold Medal at the San Francisco World Spirits Competition.

The vodka is smooth and soft because it's mineral free and has a structure that holds the delicate flavours together (Jason says his favourite part of the whole exercise is naturally the tasting – proof that not only is he a great farmer, he's also good fun). They call Black Cow 'the smoothest vodka in the world', and it's been winning awards, gaining widespread distribution in grocery, the top restaurants in London and it's being promoted by mixologists.

Black Cow co-founders are Jason Barber himself and Paul 'Archie' Archard (artist, production designer and commercials director). Jason says Archie's drive and creative flair have fuelled the momentum and trajectory of Black Cow. They have raised

£1 million for 20 per cent of the business so far, but the brand is still a side-line to the farm (Love British Food Blog, 2019).

The pivot question now is, where next? There are a series of issues. Specifically, do they extend their presence in the United States where they have some distribution? How big could they be or do they want to be? And there are a whole raft of things to address relating to culture, governance and, of course, invest-ment issues. Being successful and getting so much momentum plus comments, like that of the food critic Tom Parker Bowles who says Black Cow is one of the most remarkable things he's ever drunk, might make them feel ready to go for broke.

But beware. There are some nasty, ferocious fish out there in the drinks business.

BRYAN CLOVER'S STORY: FROM SUPPLIER TO GLOBAL EXPERT AND THOUGHT LEADER

This is the story of an old-fashioned family business. It was a classic engineer's merchant. When the founder died the family had to work out what to do with the business. It was 1996; CIS employed nine people; it turned over £0.9m. By 2018 it employed 55 people, turned over £14.5m and was highly profitable.

How this happened was the result of a careful plan and a lot of patience. The thing about family businesses is that all the family has to be enrolled in any change of strategy. The strength of family businesses is their inherent conservatism and their memory of the past. The conservatism is also of course their potential weakness. The first part of the plan related to people – staff, customers, family. The most critical person was, of course, Clover himself who had been with the business for a long time, was intensely loyal to it and would, by the nature of things, be difficult to persuade there was a different or a better way of doing things. He had to be empowered to discover that better way by himself without being told by someone else.

Rachel Bell, who was the Chairperson and whose father's company it had been, recognized Clover knew everything and that she knew virtually nothing about the intricacies of the day-to-day business (fortunately her sister, having stayed close to the business, knew quite a lot and was a key player in what followed). What Rachel did know was how to help create vision and what levers to pull to improve CIS's commercial performance. She knew it needed to pivot. The family agreed to create an EMI MBO for Clover to purchase 30 per cent of the equity, as this would incentivize him and properly reward him for taking the business to places it had not yet been. The vision of growth, the sort of growth that was actually achieved over 20 odd years was discussed, and the need to get all the key staff on side and excited was seen as the priority. Moving to a new prestigious building made a big difference in demonstrating the family's intention for the future.

Next, and progressively, the way in which the company behaved towards its customers changed from being less than just a supplier of engineering material and more a business partner and consultant. This became more than words when a state-of-the-art proving centre was set up so the business could deliver lightning fast try-it-and-see-it parts engineering. This also allowed the business to, by definition, become a proactive inno-vative force for their customers. All this allowed the business to get closer to customers and understand not just what they wanted now but also what they needed next. Finally, the customer profile began to change as customers with more prestigious reputations and bigger turnovers were attracted. And so busi-ness became more proficient and more ambitious. The proving centre has been the most important key to growth, but two other things to do with the culture of the business have also changed.

First, the planning cycle. Most small businesses live hand to mouth, which is one of the reasons they stay small. At CIS there are always one or more two- to four-year projects in the pipe-line. The business began to look to the future and become a thought leader and guide as to what in their field was going to come next.

Second, thinking the unthinkable and working on concepts like making CIS a 24/7/365 business and trialling satellite stock-vending machines, thereby reducing the need for van delivery.

Clover obviously has a sense of ownership of this reinvention of the business and is calm and self-critical in the way he regards the business. All the things he regrets relate to his late-in-life epiphany on financial control and investment creativity. He concedes he might have been quicker off the mark on liberating capital to invest in growth. Finally, he would, if he could do it all again, have sought and been helped by having better non-executive financial help. He says, looking back at the old Bryan, he can't recognize himself and realizes just how much more aspirational and margin conscious he's become since 1996.

The family and Clover have determined they have reached a point in the life of the business where an exit should be explored. They've reached a new pivot point. What he says is the business is now in great shape to buy, being well managed and full of potential. The last words belong to Clover and are the thoughts of someone seeing the bigger picture:

> We all need to spend more time looking at the future if we want to shape it. Change is constant, normal and good news so long as you have a long-term vision.

STEVE CRANFORD, NEW YORK: THE UNKNOWN WILL HIT US IN THE FACE EVERY DAY

Cranford started his life in the Mid-West of the United States. No one in his family had a business background. He trained as a lawyer after university and became a tax lawyer, following which he became a litigator in the Estates Attorney Office. At 38 he decided he needed 'to do more than just a proper job'. He also had an overwhelming urge to be an owner of a business. He describes this moment as an act of faith – 'a jump off a cliff' moment – knowing that you'll land but are not sure quite where or how. He describes entrepreneurship (which he now teaches at university) as being a bit like landing on the moon.

His first pivot (and adventure) was in retail, a furniture and electronics rent-to-own company called Rent-A-Centre. In helping position the business, he was key to successfully selling it. This was his first real experience of the emotional power of words in a sales situation. He learnt that:

- Being in a senior role in a business demands the skill of taking the initiative – being, as he puts it, 'the man'.
- There's a need to set aside the quest for perfection. You have three tools – a button to push (unless you push it nothing happens), a tiller to steer the business and an on-off switch. These are *your* tools alone.
- You have to embrace risk and ambiguity. Business is never quite as simple as you'd like. You have to be comfortable with that.
- If you're an entrepreneur, you have to understand the value of cash.

Let's pivot again. His second venture sprang from his learning from his first one of the value of communication. Stories (pictures and words) really impact on business growth. This realization, which dawned on him when selling Rent-A-Centre, led him to form an advertising agency in LA. His whole life in the legal profession and retail, he realized, had been about telling stories clearly and powerfully so as to engage an audience and persuade them to your point of view. Whisper was the agency. Here's its pitch:

> Everything you do creates conversation…audiences are naturally attracted to those who define the story of an industry so you must own the conversation within your market.

Eventually the agency pivoted geographically and moved to New York (because that's the capital of advertising conversations). Cranford says he loves the various pivots in his life: legal, retailer, ad man, strategic communication, academic (he is an established lecturer at the Creative Talent University NYC.) Here are the words of a pivot master:

> I love what I do because I know the unknown is going to hit me in the face every day...I tell clients all the time that we'll challenge all the assumptions they've had.

KIRSTIN FURBER: A PIVOT ON TOP OF A PIVOT – HOW TO NAVIGATE CHANGE

Kirstin has become something of an HR rock star, having been HR head or in a senior role at many significant media companies, BBC, 20th Century Fox, Discovery and earlier in her life, Warner. She was head of HR at BBC Worldwide, the commercial arm of the BBC, run by Tim Davie, a one-time graduate trainee at P&G and VP at PepsiCo.

From a distant perspective we'd always imagined the satirical show *W1A*, which the BBC created in 2014, was an accurate depiction of a slow-moving, politically correct institution bedded in the past. But the creation of globally lucrative properties like *CBeebies*, *Sherlock* and *Blue Planet* have changed the BBC's global image.

Kirstin has always been an exponent of creating can-do, creative cultures. She believes in the simple truths that make all the difference: 'if people are happy and encouraged to be their best selves they will perform at their very best'.

So she was enthusiastic about leading the people function in a recent start-up, the credit rating fintech, ClearScore. ClearScore had been formed in 2015 by Justin Basini who had extensive experience in marketing at Deutsche Bank and Capital One before becoming a serial entrepreneur. ClearScore was a very different world from the BBC, being full of smart, millennial techies who had great independence of spirit. The atmosphere was cutting edge. After three months, as was normal for them, the company voted on whether people should stay with the business. We asked how she felt about this. Whilst acknowledging it was uncomfortable, she said it reflected the fresh, fearless and open spirit of the company.

Her big role was going to be masterminding the integration in the forthcoming merger with Experian. ClearScore had 200 people and 8 million users and had very quickly become number two to Experian in the UK, whilst Experian was 23 years old, turned over US $4.5 billion and had 15,000 people. But the merger did not happen. The UK regulator stopped it on the basis that it would create a near monopoly in the UK and, strangely, that 'it would stifle the development of digital products'.

Kirstin decided there wasn't a big enough job for her, so she's left and will pivot into another business or create a start-up or something else exciting. She is neither demoralized nor surprised, just philosophical about what might happen next. She quotes Justin Basini, 'There are exciting times ahead'.

Minor pivoting or just refining

The art of reinvention

The tension between pivoting and perseverance, and between stability and change, are the leitmotifs of modern business. Modern marketeers seem to constantly tinker with their brands, forever producing new pack designs and new advertising campaigns. It's easy (often unnecessary) to change a pack but much more interesting and difficult to innovate and introduce a new product.

The tension between pivoting and perseverance, and between stability and change, are the leitmotifs of modern business.

Chris Wilkins, the one-time Creative Director of the advertising agency Young & Rubican, once spoke at a marketing conference about a formerly great brand called Harvey's Bristol Cream. He diagnosed a brand that, through constant changes, had become, as he put it, paranoid, schizophrenic and then 'simply took leave of its senses' when it was inexplicably positioned as a young person's drink. Anyone really experienced in marketing is, by nature, quite conservative when it comes to relaunching a brand. There aren't very many success stories for relaunches, apart from Guinness.

Successful reinvention depends (as we know) in having one foot rooted in the history and the past successes of the brand, rather than starting with a blank sheet of paper. It requires what ad man Robin Wight called 'brand archaeology'. The kindergarten of marketing taught us that 'new improved' was a very potent message; note – not 'new and completely changed'. Thus, the Royal Edinburgh Military Tattoo that officially launched in 1950 to audiences of some 6,000 is now seen by live audiences of 250,000 and in 2018 was broadcast on TV to 40 countries with audiences of around 200 million. In the next few years it's planned to take it physically to Australia and Canada and who knows where next? Peter Lederer, its Chairman, obviously does. This is history brought to new life.

Brighton Pier is the UK's most popular, free visitor attraction outside London and the fourth most popular in the UK in terms of visitor numbers. It has managed to retain its old-fashioned, English seaside feel whilst improving the visitor experience to 2019 professional standards. It's less candyfloss and more triple-cooked chips with dip-in Béarnaise sauce now. It's a brilliant job of retaining key product values but applying a pivot to 'polish, paint and people'. Staff turnover is remarkably low for the sector and training is very good, not perhaps something cynics might expect.

This is not a complete reinvention so much as a nudge in the right direction or what might be called a 'frictionless pivot'.

The Tootle story: pivoting to simplicity

Al Taylor has created several successful businesses but, as he reflected in an article for *Small Business Heroes*, in January 2019:

> [m]ost founders write a business plan that…has assumptions on who customers are, how to find them, the cost of acquiring them and how they behave – but it's not until you launch the business you discover the reality.

Tootle is a peer-to-peer used car marketplace, helping people sell their car privately but removing all the hassle (payment transaction, vetting customers, ensuring the car's mechanically sound, etc). It sounds sensible, but after a few months it became clear three things were wrong:

1 It was very expensive acquiring customers.
2 There are inexplicably no private buyers for certain cars.
3 It took a lot more customer support than expected to complete a sale.

There was too much to do here to save the business based on this model. So Al pivoted. The proposition was simplified. Now Tootle helps people find a trade buyer (car dealer or car buying service) for their car. Sellers simply enter their car details and the network of over 250 dealerships and car buying services is invited to make offers for their vehicle.

The cost of customer acquisition has fallen. The cost of servicing customers has fallen. Transactions have increased, and the business is overall much easier to manage because it's much simpler.

Remember: being right might not be enough

Mel Brooks' film, *The Producers*, was based on the idea that the Internal Revenue Service never investigated the finances of theatrical flops as they weren't expected to make money. The film is about two guys who decided to create a monster flop with heavy investment that they could embezzle and the IRS would never know. The show was called *Springtime for Hitler*. The trouble was it became a huge hit. As they realize this they say, what we think is a wonderful line too seldom used in business, 'what did we do right?'

Sometimes winning needs as much analysis as failing. Before we think of pivoting we have to know exactly what we're pivoting from and what elements of the business remain essential. In the case of Tootle, the insight that consumers want a better and simpler way of selling their car was spot on. The process Tootle had originally settled on was too complex. The pivot towards simplicity is a case, potentially, of not only seeing the opportunity but of presenting the solution in the right way.

Trends and revolutions

Central to the thesis of this book is we're witnessing a revolution in business. What this means is that to survive, let alone succeed, we need to be agile, open-minded and able to change our minds when circumstances change. Hence the significance of being able to pivot. Al Taylor gives us some thought-provoking statistics from the Start-Up Genome report of 2018:

To survive, let alone succeed, we need to be agile, open-minded and able to change our minds when circumstances change.

- Seventy-four per cent of companies failed because they tried to grow too fast. Or, put slightly differently, tried to scale up before the product, presentation and business model were completely right.
- Businesses that pivoted once or twice raised two-and-a-half times more money and were half as likely to scale up prematurely than those who didn't pivot or pivoted only once.

We conclude from this that learning through change creates one of the most potent conditions of start-up success (and that, to contradict what we said earlier, you can almost certainly turn the other cheek more than once).

But we do not live in a perfect world. We are involved in a moving-ball game where we, as a start-up, are only partially in control of events. It's how we deal with those unexpected events that matters most.

Being pivoted by external events

The words of Zach Rosner, the co-founder of Lagom, the kitchen appliance start-up in the United States, resonate when he was asked what could precipitate failure. He confessed being congenitally pessimistic, although in this instance he thought they had a good idea that was being executed well. However, as he said in an interview with us, 'there's no guarantee (of success) because so much is outside our control, not least competitive activity'.

In the current fast-changing world we have to recognize how to react and modify our behaviour in response to change. Our world has been disrupted by globalization, digital, AI, economic crises, political crises and the harsh spotlight of media – social and conventional – on all businesses. John Eustace identifies one change so rapid in its emergence that whilst we were blinking it had occurred. He said in a telephone interview with us, 'people used to make a lot of money from apps. Now they're ideas that developers steal, modify and market'.

It's become difficult to forecast change although it's never been easy (Sam Goldwyn, the film tycoon, once said, 'never make forecasts, especially about the future'). We are now living in the middle of a play that few scriptwriters would dream of writing. Many people seem to believe that things are so serious that humour no longer seems appropriate and the political figures of today are, quite simply, beyond satire. But we are better than that. We are creators of our own small comedies, and so long as they attract big enough audiences, we're laughing too.

Sometimes we get carried away by events, when the momentum of a fashion or an investment boom blinds most people to the downside of a craze. They are quite simply immune to the idea of pivoting. Things seem to be going too right to make that seem reasonable. That's what happened in the build-up to the *US housing bubble* during the 2000s, which Michael Lewis writes about in his 2010 book *The Big Short: Inside the Doomsday Machine*. A few investors resisted the general rush towards the CDO Bubble (Collateralized Debt Obligation Bubble) and became rich and unpopular, and were, until they were shown to be right, loudly derided. Pivoting against and in the face of popular opinion requires great courage and self-belief. Michael Lewis's book is a testimony to the need to be constantly and healthily sceptical. Just because virtually everyone thinks something is true is no guarantee that they're right.

Trends, readjustments and disruptions

Even if we are in the throes of a revolution, not everything will change, neither will all changes that occur be permanent. Pendulums swing backwards and then forwards. We are extremely resistant to extremist views. A current example is the misguided notion that e-books would kill paper books (they clearly haven't) or that the smartphone has changed the way people can work (what needs to change perhaps is the way people use their phones).

There are, however, three changes that we see as fundamental to the way that business is operating globally and that affect everyone:

THERE HAS BEEN A CULTURAL PIVOT IN THE THINKING OF BIG COMPANIES

They realize the need to be more observant of the cultures and behaviour of small, successful start-ups. For example, PwC,

Deloitte, McKinsey, Omnicom, Cap Gemini and others are starting their own small business units and advisory services for start-ups within their own big businesses. Increasingly, there is a recognition that whilst the big, rich and experienced can produce incomparably efficient processes, their scale alone is not enough.

The 'David and Goliath' story still holds good. For example, Schroders has taken a stake in Qwil Messenger, the first fintech start-up to have joined its global in-residence programme. As Dr Sharon Varney at Henley Business School notes, the micro-mavericks are making bigger waves. Hitherto, market-leading giants who've seemed unshakeable are under pressure on a series of fronts. Companies like Tesco, Tetra Pak, Barclays, BP and VW are not only vulnerable, their very size makes them, like dinosaurs, potentially less fit to carry on thriving in this disruptive world.

THE OLD METHODS MAY ALSO BE WRONG

Many business schools, for instance, traditionally use case studies as the best way of teaching people how to succeed in business. The trouble is so many of these case studies are based on the exploits of yesterday's heroes when the world was a different place. We should hardly recommend using the Royal Bank of Scotland as a role model for acquisition strategy now, but in the early 2000s they were the shiny role model.

Lisa Matthews (co-founder of Our Canary) was asked by a successful businessman (and we can imagine the tone of voice in which he said this), 'Where's your up-to-date business plan and your Gantt chart?'

She says she caustically replied that by the time she'd produced these the world would have moved on so fast as to make them irrelevant. She might have added that Gantt charts being 2D and, worse than that, linear, are no longer really fit for purpose in a 3D cyclical world.

THE CHANGES IN SOCIETY AND MARKETS ARE MOSTLY EXCITING, BENEFICIAL AND WEALTH CREATING

In his 2018 book, *21 Lessons for the 21st Century,* Yuval Noah Harari has a subheading in his chapter on 'Work', which is 'From exploitation to irrelevance', which we find a bleak assessment of the future of work. And we think he's wrong.

Because in a world where, hitherto, the big have been remorselessly getting bigger, we are beginning to see a movement towards more small start-ups and more people exploiting change. What could be more relevant than that? We feel the need for a quieter, healthier world. Hence the rebellion against fossil fuel and plastics. Hence the movement towards more vegetable and less meat consumption. Hence the changes in attitude to management, to gender and politics, and thus to an increasingly sceptical, populist questioning of, up until recently, unchallenged social media power.

The voice of the people has become louder, more insistent and so significant that we could call this 'the populist pivot'. As it grows in intensity, small businesses have new opportunities, targeting what niche groups really want and need. Big businesses, in contrast, thinking with the mindset of mass marketeers, create products that no one dislikes but no one loves very much either.

'New improved' describes the wave of new businesses starting and about to start.

This is just the beginning

In his 2015 book, *DISRUPT YOU! Master personal transformation, seize opportunity, and thrive in the era of endless innovation,* Jay Samit, who's the Independent Vice Chairman of Deloitte, says this:

> Pivoting is not the end of the disruption process but the beginning of the next leg of your journey.

Thinking about the start-up process as a journey captures the entrepreneurial pilgrimage. It's a journey with various stops for refreshment and reflection and occasionally a change in the route, because detours can be instructive or because there's a roadblock ahead. We particularly like the thought of 'an era of endless innovation', which might be a subtitle for our book because current conditions have created a climate of finding more and unthought-of new ways of doing things and doing them better, faster, cheaper and in ways that engage consumers.

It's just the beginning, but, as Kirstin Furber said, there are exciting times ahead.

CHAPTER FOUR

Pop-ups, questions and experiments

What is a pop-up?

Let's start by taking a quick look at what a pop-up is, beginning with the history of pop-ups.

The history

Pop-ups started in 1298 in Vienna when their citizens were allowed to set up temporary December markets. At the end of the 20th century, the concept was reinvented and the pop-up became a well-known concept. It has always been a bit of a casual affair – a get-together rather than a meeting; a happening rather than an event. Popping in or popping out is not something planned in the diary; popping up to a nearby city or popping over to see grandparents is no big deal, and it's this that makes the concept feel so spontaneous and contemporary.

We live in a world where consumers are increasingly promiscuous and brand loyalty cannot be counted upon. 'One-off tactical projects' are the activities that dominate the current business world rather than strategic campaigns. Increasingly, our working lives are more focused on tactics than strategy and are more to do with sales than brand building. In the past, in advertising or PR, we were very often regarded as the guardians of brand values or the stewards of strategy. Now the priority is to be a driver of sales. All these changes have altered our priorities. When we're going to be mainly judged by our results on a quarterly basis, there is a lesser need for visions written in stone. We are looking instead for 'killer points of immediate competitive difference' and for super tactical agility. We are looking for pop-up goals rather than great ball control.

We live in a world where consumers are increasingly promiscuous and brand loyalty cannot be counted upon.

This is a pop-up world where we constantly create pop-up concepts (which are also called 'strawmen'). We are, or should be, constantly looking to explore a variety of approaches to problems to see which are likely to be the most effective.

Pop-ups as key tactical tools

Pop-ups come in many forms, but in their simplest format they're about swiftly assessing the commercial viability of a business concept, a new product, a series of marketing variables or the lowest cost and best way of delivering a product or service. We can think of a pop-up as creating a real-life laboratory rather than a theoretical test-bed.

The pop-up is a tactical tool, not just a cheap way of retailing. It allows us to check on different and new ideas, messages or presentational approaches. What used to be an expensive, laborious and rather slow affair called a 'test market', is now a swift, cheap hothouse, where a business owner can see the whites of their customers' eyes as they try the products on offer and then, hopefully, buy them.

The role of technology and innate curiosity

Technology has helped us. 3D modelling allows potential customers to be shown a seemingly 'real' product that's cheap and quick to produce. CIS – the engineering business – created a 'proving centre' where they could simply produce a new part and say 'you mean like this? Yes, it could be like this, or you could try this instead'. What starts as a pop-up demonstration becomes a sales conversation. Everyone does it now. British comedian Michael McIntyre gathers people, friends and fearless critics together and tries out lots of new jokes and sketches. What looked good on paper may bomb in front of an audience, and it's better to find that out in a sitting room than at the Gotham Comedy Club in New York, The Comedy Store, Sydney, or the Apollo Hammersmith, London.

Restaurants have pop-ups or, in the case of a new restaurant they have soft openings, to find out how well their gastronomic story is received, how rapturously their dishes are devoured or, alternatively, are left on the side of the plate.

In 16th-century Venice, the artist Tintoretto tested the effects of light by making small wax models of figures and putting them in a box into which candlelight was shone, enabling him to see how alternating postures created different shadows. This was much more illustrative and realistic than experimenting on canvas. It was a Renaissance pop-up.

Thinking in new, experimental ways

In a Deloitte article (Think Forward Initiative, 2019), Daniel Gilbert, Harvard psychologist, professor and author of the 2007 *New York Times*' bestselling book *Stumbling on Happiness*, says, 'We are only now learning to think in beta, which is the best way of planning for the future'. Although we've been around for millions of years, the software in our brains that allows us to think forward, or plan for the future, is actually quite 'new'. Pop-ups allow us to see what happens to ideas in practice where we can make adjustments, learn as we go and create our future at low cost.

Google and others have been trying out semi-driverless cars, for instance, for a long time, but we are now getting close to fully driverless presences on our roads. In the meantime, we have countless pop-up trials because reality, not theory, is the only proper testing zone.

The world of business is shifting from long boring meetings where participants lose interest, their attention strays and they become demotivated. Increasingly, shorter, more creative interventions, kick-offs and conferences are being set up, designed not just to communicate but also to inspire people. The UK conference market was estimated to be worth £18 billion in 2017. That's a lot of money to spend on boring people. Pop-up events seem increasingly the way to go.

Overall, today's business climate is one where trial and error and quick feedback are essential to gain competitive advantage. The better and more adventurous the pop-up culture within a business, the greater the chance of success. In the case of start-up businesses, the extensive use of pop-up trials is axiomatic to rolling out a product, or business offering, on a more serious basis.

Nothing beats talking to real people and seeing our life's work being noticed (being noticed is a good start), being considered (that's even better), being tried and loved or hated by the potential customer, or, finally, being tried and then being tried again (and this is when we really feel like a winner). And don't we now know a lot more than we did before and haven't we learnt what changes, if any, need to be made?

Nothing beats authentic feedback, which, at relatively low cost, is what a pop-up trial will give us.

Pop-ups in action

By definition a tech start-up is a pop-up

The failure rate of tech start-ups is very high (according to an article in *Fast Company* by Faisal Hoque, it's around 75 per cent). Tech businesses fail because they aren't original enough or, if they are original, they're not quite good enough. Ben Horowitz, in his 2014 book *The Hard Thing about Hard Things*, suggests that if you aren't 10 times better than what's already on offer, then you won't win. Alternatively, your business model may be one in which customer recruitment is too expensive or, especially in the tech sector, you are too slow to market because, most of all, this is a market sector so competitive that even if you spot an opportunity, the chances are someone else will spot it just minutes later.

But if you have invented the world's most distinctive and delicious jam, you have time to refine it and make it even more delicious. In high tech you are playing ice hockey against the best and you have to be where the puck is going to be next, not where it is now. Reid Hoffman says the biggest mistake that entrepreneurs in the tech space make is to minimize risk rather than focus on the 'live-or-die' bet. They are by definition treading in unknown areas, where understanding how to maximize the chance of success is dependent on high speed pivots that you can do in a pop-up but that in start-up mode are harder and much more expensive. *Blitz scale* are the words Hoffman and others use to describe really going for it. One thing is clear in this space. You win or you don't exist. You can't be a nice, little tech company. In his book, Horowitz describes this world of the unknown in which there's no recipe for really dynamic, difficult and unique situations.

Theoretically, starting a tech company isn't that different from starting a food company except in terms of the speed of thinking and the quick action needed. Both have wheels, but, here's the crux of the story, one is a bicycle and the other is a Formula One car. This means a hot executive with great experience in one is often struggling in the other. Perhaps that's why, in the end, John Sculley, who'd been a huge success at PepsiCo, found running Apple so difficult. He nearly said 'no' to joining them until seduced by a line that demonstrates what a great salesman Steve Jobs was. Sculley mentions it in the documentary *Bloomberg Game Changers: Steve Jobs:* 'Do you want to sell sugar water for the rest of your life, or do you want to come with me and change the world?'

A pop-up story

The story of the 'Sussex Peasant' pop-up

We first realized that Edward Johnstone might be a bit special when he became the manager at a café/bar called 'The Cyclist' at Brighton station. Station restaurants are usually terrible places that ought to be ashamed of themselves. Well, The Cyclist was a cracking bar-bistro terminus station watering hole. It was decorated with wit and style with the bar created by sticking lots of old suitcases together. The beer was local with constant pop-up guest beers, so it was always interesting. The whole place was a pop-up delight.

What happened next was a tragedy. In 2017 Southern Rail and the RMT Union declared war on each other and, with the constant strikes, the London Victoria to Brighton line became something of a graveyard for commuter careers. The Cyclist was shut down as their thirsty commuter-customers stopped drinking on their way home because they drove to work, camped out in London or vowed never to travel by train again.

Johnstone, who'd previously been a head hunter in the City of London recruiting traders and market analysts with their eye-watering packages, had a calling to start his own business and change the world. So, he emerged in a different guise driving a converted horsebox with a new venture called the 'Sussex Peasant', a pop-up food retailer selling fruit, meat and vegetables only grown and raised in Sussex farms. Edward believes in a green, self-sufficient world where we eat better, fresher and more locally. There was a village in Central France where the mayor erected a placard that proclaimed, 'eat the food grown and raised here in this village we love'. This could have been Johnstone talking.

His vision is to transform our food supply chain by creating communities who prefer the delicious taste of local, farmed food. Currently, he claims only 1 per cent of what we eat in Sussex is grown in Sussex. He started this venture with five farm suppliers that have grown to 15 (and he's looking for more.)

The visible symbol of local, countryside authenticity lies in that horsebox, which he parks in four strategic places between Friday and Monday around Brighton. The antique horsebox is the perfect image of British farmland. A second and third horsebox are now in operation, increasing his Brighton and Hove reach. He reckons in time just four horseboxes will give him enough coverage of Sussex. And then? The Kent, Surrey and Hampshire Peasants come next.

The integrated concept of local farmers and a clientele that cares about food that actually tastes better is given a uniquely *local* polish. Ed also picks up local gems of home-made produce – Suzy's Streat Food preserves and Smorl's humous (is this the best humous ever produced?).

A few people say it's rather expensive, but this is fine if the taste bonus is consistent and noticeable; the loyal shoppers think it is. The graduation from pop-up to start-up has happened, but the scale-up across Sussex will need some smart logistics and management. It has plenty of energy and self-belief already. Here's hoping this 'returning food and drink to what it once was' business continues to deliver. Our world needs better food. Our world needs to eat more locally produced produce. Our world needs more Eds.

We need to be fizzy, busy and buzzy

We sometimes underestimate the extent to which establishing a new relationship with a person or in creating a start-up is like plunging into ice cold water. Lori H Gordon in *Psychology Today* says that intimate relationships are decreasing. It also seems that more and more young people may prefer to start, and even prolong, a relationship online rather than face to face. Good (maybe) for pop-up relationships and for beginning to get to know someone but not so good for, say, marriage. All pop-up. No start-up.

Video games like Fortnite engage the young (there are over 200 million players worldwide). Skills are learnt. Relationships are forged. We are creating a lot of clever, agile but, at the same time, shy and introverted people. And in starting a business, a solo existence working from a bedsit, with Caffè Nero as the nearest 'office', won't do. Ultimately, if we're starting a business, we need to be able to sell and get a sense of the competition and think about and understand our customers. In other words, we need to mix with real people. Sitting in that bedsit on our own is not going to make us a persuasive, agile, responsive and thinking business owner.

And that's where co-working spaces come into their own and help turn cautious hermits into gregarious winners. Platf9rm in Brighton and Hove, as we've described, has many assets. But three are key: a sense of *design* that has wit and style; the *noisy hum* of success and a real sense of *community*. Imagine the market square in a county town on market day, imagine the coffee bar in a busy creative business. Such places inspire collaborative thinking.

Now watch the 200 or so people bustling around Platf9rm and you could imagine saying to yourself 'one day I'll be running a business that feels just like this – *fizzy, busy and buzzy*'. Running your 'still in beta' business in a place like this gives you a sense of being 'in it' and 'with it' together with others, not being out there on your own.

Incidentally, we need to avoid confusing 'pop-up' with 'not to be taken seriously'. In a pop-up world of speed dating, swiping right is all that anyone talks about. If we want to call our pop-up business something with more gravitas, let's call it a 'beta concept trial', but everyone will know it's really still a pop-up. And that really is OK, especially if we're busy out there in the real world, talking and laughing with real people and behaving like a player, rather than a spectator.

Pop-ups are changing the way we sell

Think back. The retail world used to be neatly structured with important big department stores like British Home Stores and House of Fraser, Safeway and Fine Fare in grocery, and independent specialists like Gumps and Brookstone in the United States and Maplins and Oddbins in the UK. All are gone. Mark Twain said, 'The rumours of my death have been greatly exaggerated', but rumours about the death of the high street have persisted legitimately. The assassin is variously, over time, identified as being out-of-town developments, online competition, the economy...or all three. What has become increasingly popular are pop-ups in the form of concessions, or small stages for a piece of retail theatre, in the few remaining big department stores.

But the real pop-up adventures are occurring behind the high street in London's Soho or Covent Garden, New York's Chelsea, Sydney's Manly Market and in the UK, Tunbridge Wells' Pantiles, York's Shambles or Brighton's North Laine. This is where experiments and eccentric ideas emerge and flourish. This is where people wander rather than drive, try unusual drinks and food, discover unusual stationery and fashion outlets, or pubs that offer 60 different brands of gin.

Alternatively, you can go to a named local hotel, anywhere in the UK, on a given date and be measured up by an expert for a Sam's Suit, your measurements being emailed to a factory in

Hong Kong where they start work at once and you pick up your suit a week later or, if you're in Hong Kong, 24 hours later. Pop-up designer fashion bargains appear regularly in TK Maxx with their Gold Label offerings on the 'Gold Rail'...but hurry. You'll find similar experiences in Marshalls and Winners in the United States and Canada. This is speed pop-up.

There are free trial offers (should we call them pop-up-trials?) on mattresses. In 2018 and 2019, a 'mattress war' was started with price cuts and all the online brands like Casper, Emma and Eve offering 100 nights' free trial of the mattress and the promise they will pick it up 'if you decide you don't like it'. We recall the distant past when the mail order catalogues tried something similar but to ill effect. The worst area was wedding dresses. There were huge returns of lipstick- and champagne-stained wedding dresses with return notes saying, 'not required'. Pop-ups come and go, but cock-ups are constant.

Understanding markets and people

Let's talk about the audience as boss

In the excitement of creating something new, a product, a service, an app, a new dish, a book, a play, a film or a piece of music, we can sometimes forget there's an audience out there. However good what we've done may be, it has to engage and excite people enough to buy it. The US actor Sean Evans said, 'Ultimately, my boss is the audience'. He's also compere of *The Hot Ones*, where he interviews people as they eat progressively hotter and hotter spices on chicken wings.

The theatre as pop-up

We're interested in the ultimate pop-upness of live theatre. Whilst it costs between £200k and £400k to put on a professional play, and enough money and free time to make anyone think twice about putting on an amateur production, there's a bloodthirsty ruthlessness that accompanies London West End or Broadway productions. Extras and smaller parts are despatched without compunction if a production's audiences fall off. The audience figures run everything – *La Strada,* a Lionel Bart musical, closed on Broadway after just one show. Even blockbusters like *The Book of Mormon* at the Prince of Wales London, which has been running since 2011, is run very tightly with a small, multitasking cast, several of whom can play many parts. When a pop-up becomes a staple (and few do), it becomes a cash cow, but, interestingly, theatrical pop-ups never seem to scale up. In fact, over time, they tend to reduce in size as the cast members and backstage staff become more adept at their tasks and thus more 'productive'.

There are over 1,300 theatres in the UK (240 major ones in London) and an astonishing 22 million people go to the theatre every year – over 50 per cent more than go to watch Premier League football. Yes, this is, by definition, a pop-up business. And a very big one.

Mary Allen, arts expert and theatrical doyen

After being Secretary General of the Arts Council in the early 1990s, Mary became General Director of the Royal Opera House, in effect bailing out the operation at a moment of architectural change, when her predecessor resigned owing to ill health. Her tenure was a sad example of how the clash of arts, business and politics can lead to discord and a climate in which cogent management is impossible. She alone came out of the debacle with credit saving the 'House' from extinction. Her legacy is the best Opera House in the world. So, a pop-up appointment didn't work out for her, on a personal level, but it worked well for ballet and opera in the long run.

Her talent now as a poet and theatrical director includes the deliciously named Doyly Tarts at Aldeburgh in Suffolk, which has raised £15k a year for charity with their plays. She teaches us about the real pop-up and how the process of getting it on stage works. Here's the story as it unfolds:

- You have a play...but just on paper...it reads quite well.
- The director reads it, thinks hard and creates an interpretation and feel for it...a working plan.
- The director needs to find players – the casting session is long, tricky...and tearful.
- The director/cast collaboration creates a working plan that becomes an action plan; this part is about 'building the story' and bringing it to life.
- The production manager takes over – they are, says Mary, the real CEOs controlling all the elements from budget control to marketing to making the creative vision work on stage.

As a pop-up, a theatrical show is created on the move with life being breathed into it as it transforms from idea to reality, to success or failure. And all of that success or failure depends on the boss. The audience.

Film as pop-ups facing disruption

Film is not really pop-up in the same way, because the big money is spent before the audience gets its say. And the boss (the audience) is unforgiving and fickle. But by examining this industry, we can see it resembles the way the world at large is developing. It's been disrupted by technology, new business models, leaders who've gone from heroes to zeros, start-ups, pivots and lots of flops and catastrophic misjudgements. *John Carter*, the 2012 Disney sci-fi extravaganza starring Taylor Kitsch, cost US $263 million to make and lost US $122 million.

In the 1950s in the UK over a billion admissions to cinema were recorded annually, but over the following 60 years the cinema went into long, interminable decline for all kinds of reasons. There has been a decline in creative productions, the demise of Hollywood, the rise of TV and then, most recently, the arrival of compelling new competition on TV from HBO, Amazon, Netflix, now Apple and others. This decline was arrested in 2018 with a slight recovery to the best admission figures for a decade. Meanwhile, in India, Bollywood, and in Nigeria, Nollywood, are both much bigger than Hollywood in output and are rewriting all the rules. An average Hollywood film spends a year in production and costs around US $65 million to make; in Nigeria production takes less than 10 days and costs around US $10,000. In a global context all bets are off with comparisons like that. Good diverse stories come from all over the place now. *Black Panther*, the top grossing film out of Hollywood in 2018, shifted the dial of change even further, as did Netflix's *Roma* with a huge clutch of awards and the biggest Oscar nominations for a film not in English.

Ask Adam Spence or Ian George (ex-Warner, Pathé, 20th Century Fox, Paramount and now Sony) about the film industry and they'll say this is the most unpredictable, expensive, opinionated, rough (but also thrilling) business that there is. A business where you are only as good as your last film. Ian tells the story when he was at Pathé and was convinced when offered *The Blair Witch Project* in 1999 that it was going to be a catastrophe. He admits he was wrong because it cost US $60 million to make and it actually grossed US $250 million. This is a vivid example of how difficult it is, even when as experienced and astute as he was, to predict success.

In that respect every single film is a very expensive pop-up.

Music is a pop-up

(IF YOU THOUGHT THE FILM INDUSTRY WAS DISRUPTED...)

It used to be so cosy in Tin Pan Alley. Do you remember the Liverpool sound, the wave of pop stars from everywhere around the UK and around the United States – from Motown to

Memphis to Nashville? The charts were something all teenagers tracked but not just teenagers – parents woke children up to tell them, '*Bird Dog*'s gone to number one, darling' – yes, pop was news and we all cared about it.

This was the world of pop-ups, as unknown groups and one-hit wonders appeared on *Top of the Pops* and *Juke Box Jury* in the UK and *American Bandstand* and *Shindig* in the United States. *New Musical Express* sold 300,000 copies in 1964. Anyone could make it, or at any rate try to make it. But the game has changed now. Music is controlled by Sony and Warner and a few others in the United States, and Spotify, Grooveshark, Pandora, the late Rdio (now owned by Pandora) and YouTube. The giants have mopped up.

It takes courage to compete. Harry Maitland has already appeared in *Start-ups, Pivots and Pop-ups*, but his is a specific pop-up story that's relevant. Harry is extremely bright, energetic and thoughtful and talks about a group, Catfish and the Bottlemen, whom he likes a lot, who started in Aberystwyth in 1997, came to prominence in 2013 but only hit the big time in 2017. So, you have to be patient. Being a pop-up can last a long time.

Harry talks about busking, which is damp, cold but can be lucrative. More to the point, for his new group, Rats, they need 'likes' on social media – because 'likes' get you gigs and they found a creative way of getting them. They drove the 220 miles from Liverpool in the North West of England to East London overnight, travelled end to end and back again on the District Line underground performing and saying, 'please no money; just give us 'likes' on social media'. It was a huge success. In this pop-up world it's more important to be liked than paid when you start.

In this pop-up world it's more important to be liked than paid when you start.

Restaurants are the perfect pop-up role models

The late Anthony Bourdain, the introduction to whose book *'Les Halles' Cookbook* is the best short advice on how to run a small, hectic, creative business we've ever read, said, 'If anything is good for pounding humility into you permanently, it's the restaurant business'. And he's right, because a restaurant is the quintessential pop-up business. It has high failure rates, poor margins, strong chances of libellous reviews by competitors, being ripped off by staff, hot and cramped working conditions and really terrible hours. And they have to keep smiling and be nice to their customers, remembering Charles Orvis's words (he founded his first fishing tackle and outdoor garment outlets in 1856 in Manchester, Vermont), 'the customer's always right even when they're goddamned wrong'.

Both of us would have been good in the hospitality business (Rachel was briefly) because in our respective businesses (advertising and PR) we took Orvis's advice to heart and remembered that just as going to a restaurant is meant to be exciting, to be deliciously memorable, in fact a bit of an adventure, so a trip to 'the agency' by a client is like a day out, a refreshing change from the normal humdrum and should be full of creative ideas, mind-opening thoughts and inspiration. The organizational structure of a restaurant from *maître d'* through to waiters and foul-tempered creative chefs has similarities to the agency model. And living in a world where our reputation is constantly on the line is also one we recognize.

Pop-ups, soft openings, gala events, promotional events are things we, in frontline marketing, live or have lived with constantly. A good example of pop-up success is Cin-Cin in Brighton, which started life as a van selling fresh pasta to Brighton Festival visitors near the Dome Concert Hall and graduated to a small counter service restaurant and then to a second rather larger counter service restaurant.

Institutionalizing pop-ups

Storefront (www.thestorefront.com/) is the parent to many pop-ups. It runs a magazine and has access to 10,000 outlets. It rhapsodizes (perhaps unsurprisingly) about pop-ups and their potential and the fact that the increasing importance of online shouldn't obscure the need for a real experiential retail presence, especially where theatre can flourish. Even Amazon has become a bricks and mortar retailer as well as retaining its online dominance. Its first physical bookstore, Amazon Books, launched in Seattle in 2015 and has since expanded across the United States. Its acquisition of Wholefoods gave it 460 stores in the United States, Canada and the UK. Finally, Amazon Go, the cashier-less grocery outlets, has now opened in the United States. This is how Amazon describes them:

> Our Just Walk Out Technology automatically detects when products are taken from or returned to the shelves and keeps track of them in a virtual cart. When you're done shopping, you can just leave the store. A little later, we'll send you a receipt and charge your Amazon account.

In the context of Amazon's scale (its turnover is some £230 billion), these Go outlets are their versions of experimental pop-ups.

The Storefront guidelines to pop-ups

Storefront, having appointed themselves as the champion and patron of pop-ups, advises people thinking of creating a pop-up shop on the seven key steps to take in their *Storefront Magazine*. We've modified and amplified it slightly, but only slightly because it's good advice:

1 Establish what you think success looks like beforehand – what do you want to get out of customers experiencing your product in the real world? Define what your success matrices are. Set targets in sales, footfall, customer feedback. Set goals.

2 Define your key value drivers – decide what the three most important things are in driving your point of difference – are people responding to those or to something else? Are your plan, product and presentation what you expected them and hoped them to be?

3 Use the digital to promote the physical – but don't just stop there. Can other digital technologies such as virtual reality, augmented reality, or digital projection be used at the pop-up store itself to increase the 'wow' factor? But don't get carried away. Don't let technology obscure your proposition.

4 Don't forget what you've already learnt – a pop-up store, whilst unique in its potential, is still a channel just like any other. Many of the same rules still apply. Remember, you are in essence creating your own little world focused on your own little brand. As such, make sure you are still watching, listening and learning. Also throw yourself into this – your personality matters – this is *your* show and as well as being a pop-up, it's your opportunity to hothouse your learning.

5 Embrace the experience – have fun. Be creative. If you are an outdoor clothing brand, let your customers try your products whilst enjoying a climbing wall. Do you sell power tools? Set up a working workshop in your pop-up so customers can actually make something with your product. If it's a drink or food, have a tasting.

6 Be a marketing scientist – using the metrics and tracking you set up ahead of time, use your pop-up shop to test as many hypotheses as you can during its run. Accept this is not a faithful replication of an ordinary retail outlet, but this enables you to be as pushy as possible in finding out what's right and what's wrong with your offering.

7 Calculate and assess – do a rigorous post-mortem on the whole initiative. Before you start your pop-up, be sure you itemize all the questions you want to be answered, and before you conclude the exercise, check them to see if any are unanswered.

Then take an overview. Having gone through everything, ask yourself three questions:

a Are you more or less confident than before you started?

b Do you know what you need to change and how to change it?

c How much money are you prepared to risk on this product now?

Brighton Gin: pop-up, check-out and have a laugh

Johnny Ray, serial author and wine writer for the weekly British magazine on politics, culture, and current affairs, *The Spectator*, is co-founder of Brighton Gin together with Nigel Lamb, ex-owner of W J King Brewery and, most importantly, Kathy Caton Managing Director and Distiller. Kathy is a radio presenter and producer for *BBC Radio 4* and other channels. This trio, and others, decided fun-loving Brighton deserved its own gin since everyone else was having a go (Camden Gin, Edinburgh Gin, Salcombe Gin and many others). Kathy, in a typical pop-up comment, says, 'gin is a forgiving spirit that gives you less bad hangovers or, in the case of Brighton organic gin, a virtually hangover free life'.

Well to be fair they decided to do things properly and did some market research. A blind tasting of 40 gin brands with 40 randomly selected gin drinkers, in a church. What did they discover? Johnny tells us that Tanqueray did well but not as well as expected and that Brighton Gin did exceedingly well. He pauses…and in a slightly strained voice adds, stifling a giggle, 'we also discovered when you drink a lot of gin you get rather drunk'.

Remember, the consumer has a sense of humour as well as a wallet.

This was pop-up research at its most involving.

It was also something else, which is too often discounted by serious business people – that the ability to have a big sense of humour and the capacity to laugh are important in a small business. Audiences want to be entertained as well as engaged and helped along in discovering a new brand. Brighton Gin with its human spirit (as well as its alcoholic spirit) shows the founders have created a joyous brand, not just a functionally excellent one.

Remember, the consumer has a sense of humour as well as a wallet.

Pop-ups as cultural phenomena

We live in tumultuous times in which businesses go into administration and pop up again under new ownership just days later. Patisserie Valerie and Smallbone kitchens in the UK were examples of this early in 2019. The certainties of survival are not as they were. Gone are the days when investors used to say, 'you can never go wrong with Marks and Spencer's, GEC and ICI', because you can and will have done if that was your chosen, stick-with-it portfolio. In this slightly chaotic environment, pop-ups are becoming more important and relevant to the current mood of the public. Here's what Nikki Baird, VP of Retail Innovation, wrote in *Forbes* Magazine:

> My sense…is that pop-ups are not fads. Like flash sales, they're not going to totally remake retail into a whole new business model but are probably going to have to become (part of) a regular, sustained effort by retailers. It will become another channel in the portfolio of customer engagement channels.

Brixton, South London: a cultural eye-opener

There are many pop-up stories. Virtually every town throughout the world has a market or a group of people doing their thing, but there's one that stands out and that's Brixton. We hadn't visited Brixton for many years. What's changed is a new confidence and abundance of activity. The State of Brixton (it seems like a State in its own right) feels very successful. However, its history is somewhat chequered. There were the Brixton Riots of 1981 and 1995 followed by the London Riots of 2011 that spread from Tottenham in North London following the police shooting of Mark Duggan. These riots spread across London, reflecting widespread discontent with alleged racial discrimination by the police and more generally with the economy and the government. Around £200 million of damage was done in London. Brixton was always central to such disturbances with a loud, angry voice.

Brixton has a diversity of race and culture. It is, to use those hackneyed words, 'vibrant and colourful'. And they have their own currency – the Brixton Pound. It's designed to support Brixton businesses and encourage local trade and production. It's a complementary, not a replacement, currency for use by independent local shops and traders. What it says about localism is powerful and it adds to the sense of 'the State of Brixton' as a standalone entity.

Get off the last stop southbound on the Victoria Line underground and you emerge into a new country – Brixton. It's like being abroad somewhere exotic. The market is crammed with butchers, fishmongers and greengrocers. There's a frenzy of food and vegetables that would not be familiar to Waitrose shoppers. From the sea and rivers: flying fish, catfish, groupers, parrot fish, pirate perch; from the soil: mamey sapote, chayote squash, boniato, jicama.

It's the noise, bustle, smell and pricing that is alien to what's going on 20 minutes up the Victoria Line. In Brixton you get a double espresso for £1.20. There's a populist cornucopia that you'd expect to find in a hot blue sky climate, not in drizzly South London. Across the road from the market is Pop Brixton. It's a community project of pop-up shops, bars and restaurant kiosks selling food from all over the world. But it's more than retail. It's a co-working community of local, creative, independent businesses too. We would love to work there but there's a snag – it would be a calorific catastrophe for us. Giles Coren, *The Times* restaurant critic and columnist, likes ramen and was gobsmacked by Pop Brixton:

> In the end we found a stand-up ramen joint called Koi and ordered a bowl of tonkotsu pork ramen to share and a plate of gyoza. And the soup was…OUTSTANDING. Worth the trip alone. A superbly rich and creamy, mouth-coating pork bone broth, really good egg noodles, a fresh soft egg and slices of pork belly. The kind of thing that makes you sing hurrah for 2017 after all, that such a bowlful can be found in a shipping container in Brixton quite by chance. And for £6!

Pop Brixton operates out of a 1,400 square foot jumble of shipping containers and has 50 businesses and stalls. Apart from Koi, there's L'Amuse Bouche (where M Croque and M Crêpes met), the World of Wurst (sausages from around the world), Alpe (Alpine food – lots of melted cheese), Studmuffin ('the muffin revolution is here'), Mama's Jerk (Mama Charlotte's secret recipe brought up to date). There are design businesses, an education company offering academic tuition to all, a little farm, a radio station, a make-do-and-mend and a restoration business. Buzzy and busy. It's as though the rest of London somehow doesn't exist.

The community spirit is what drives this collection of experimentalists, eccentrics and specialists. It started in 2015, using a disused parcel of land and the local council's encouragement. It was conceived as a genuine, temporary pop-up. But its life has been extended. It's managed by a company called Make Shift, a team of designers, entrepreneurs and architects who are taking a new approach to the way we use space in cities. The next Make Shift project, Peckham Levels, in south east London, is a disused seven-storey car park now crammed with creative workspaces, food stalls, music and community facilities. Pop Brixton and now

Peckham Levels are changing the pop-up world, taking pop-up culture to a new level. What's striking is the sheer quality and professionalism of the products served and sold there. This has no hint of a second-hand charity cast-off feel in its personality.

Localism is alive and well in a globalized world. Pop-ups rule OK.

The pop-up culture is spreading and developing

The new wave of pop-ups (now all very well-established businesses) – Amazon, Airbnb, Deliveroo and Uber – all started with a pop-up culture. Uber and Airbnb started with low capital cost entry – the cars and the apartments, houses and villas were owned by someone else. What they shared with Pop Brixton was the sense of adventure in breaking new ground and attacking tired, old, incumbent businesses – the book trade, the hotel trade, the restaurant trade and taxi businesses.

Amazon seems to employ a new pop-up breed of delivery person for the Amazon Prime extraordinary (often same day) delivery. They arrive breathless and in a clapped out second-hand car…the very essence of pop-up. Whatever we may feel about the ruthless steamroller of a business that Amazon is, we should also acknowledge its enterprise and brilliant logistics processes. They have helped drive that bar of customer service up a bit higher. More books are now being sold: in 2018 physical book sales were up 5 per cent whilst e-books slightly declined. Waterstones and a raft of bookshops have smartened up their act and begun to make the book browsing and buying experience much more enjoyable.

The same thing has happened with taxi drivers, who have become more cheerful, more courteous, accept credit cards and have less of that we-own-this-city bumptiousness. And Uber is not impervious itself. Pop-ups can get knocked down, as well as do their David act with weary Goliaths. Uber has found that out painfully in China, thanks to Didi Chuxing, and in India, by Ola Cabs. (Incidentally Didi Chuxing is now making inroads into Latin America. This Chinese company, like Alibaba, is taking our world by storm. So, watch out.)

Meanwhile, Airbnb, if it did nothing else, has shown renting operators how to photograph properties, how to describe them (in good, plain language) and how to cover all the key killer benefits in summary. It has conducted a master class in communication. It's also shown hoteliers how to maximize valuation. In early 2019, Airbnb market cap was US $38 billion; Inter-Continental Hotels Group's market cap was US $8.3 billion.

The Christmas market boom

Christmas markets have become the most popular pop-ups ever. One of the most highly rated is that at Winchester Cathedral with over 100 very smart, standardized wooden stalls selling everything from mulled wine to bratwurst to decorations, art, slippers, confectionery, jewellery and ingenious inventions and devices for opening jars. A decade ago, you had to go to Germany to find a Christmas market. Not anymore. Sleigh bells fill the air in every town in Britain.

Pop-ups are becoming more normal. Local brands are getting exposure. Start-ups, thanks to pop-ups, are getting an early foot in the door.

Pop-ups are becoming more normal. Local brands are getting exposure. Start-ups, thanks to pop-ups, are getting an early foot in the door.

Pop-ups create ideas and save money

The 'skunk works' concept (another type of pop-up)

The history of creative business pop-ups goes back to the Second World War and the development of a revolutionary Jet Fighter by Lockheed. The name 'skunk works' was taken from the comic strip *Li'l Abner*. The designation describes a group within an organization given a high degree of autonomy and unfettered by bureaucracy with the task of working on advanced or secret projects.

Lockheed's advanced development programme continued throughout the Cold War developing breakthrough designs like the U2 and Stealth Bombers. But probably the most famous skunk works was set up for IBM by Bill Lowe in Boca Raton in 1980. They said that they could develop the IBM PC within a year and they did just that. We have to see this against the background of IBM's historically slow developments and excruciating bureaucracy. According to Steven Dufresne, in an article about the IBM PC in *Hackaday*, one analyst at the time of its launch said, 'IBM bringing out a personal computer would be like teaching an elephant to tap dance'.

Lowe picked a group of 12 strategists who produced a plan for hardware, software, manufacturing set-up and sales strategy. It was so well conceived that the basic strategy remained unaltered throughout the product cycle. Better still, as the word spread about what was going on, talent and expertise were drawn in. The plan was to use tested vendor technology; create a standardized, one-model product; open architecture; and outside sales channels so as to achieve quick consumer market saturation.

The manufacturing strategy was to simplify everything. There was no time to develop and test all components. So, they shopped for completely functioning and pre-tested sub-assemblies, put them together and then tested the final product. Zero defects was part of the plan.

The development team broke all the old established IBM rules and acted as an independent business unit procuring the most appropriate and reliable parts from wherever they could. This enabled them to develop the IBM PC in 12 months – at that time that was faster than any other hardware product in IBM's history.

Are skunk works really the way forwards?

Steve Blank, in his article for *Forbes* Magazine 'Why Corporate Skunk Works Need to Die', threw scorn on the efficacy of skunk works, 'By the middle of the 21st century the only companies with skunk works will be the ones that have failed to master *continuous innovation*'.

Steve's gripe might seem legitimate; he's saying, in effect, outsourcing innovation cannot be right. Shouldn't you be doing it everywhere in your business all the time not just when asked to? Would Apple put all its innovation into a separate exclusive area? Would an advertising agency?

Well yes. That's exactly what they do. The super-creatives are kept in a cage called the 'Creative Department', whilst the executives schmooze clients, beg for more time to finish assignments and oil the wheels – rather like the Hungarian, Zoltan Karpathy, in *My Fair Lady* who was said to do this by 'oozing charm at every pore he oiled his way around the floor'.

Big organizations cannot afford to be continuously innovative. They have to have teams who are great at logistics, teams who make sure the manufacturing process has zero defects and, finally, a team who can innovate, think laterally and be ahead of the market. These are the people who must be left alone to create or, in the case of IBM, be separated from the mother culture. And, if all companies were staffed only with 'creatives', in the real sense of the word, they would go bust fast because these creatives tend to be expensive, untidy, irrational and dreamy.

The great thing about skunk works is that they are allowed to break the rules. The terrible thing about Steve's view is he thinks either they should be closely controlled or that the whole company should be like them. Leading edge creativity, like tequila, should be treated with a high degree of caution.

Pop-ups as a way of finding out what people really think and how they behave

It's interesting that as a traditional marketeer, Kellogg's has researched a new range of cereals in Europe by creating a series of pop-ups in France hosted by celebrity chefs. Apparently, it was a great success as an event but more particularly they also learnt a lot about the way, when they're relaxed, the average consumer describes how they feel about the brand and its developments. Kellogg's has a track record with pop-ups. In 2016 they opened their own pop-up cereal café in Times Square, New York. It has since closed as it was only ever envisaged as a temporary fixture. But it was so successful, a new, much bigger, permanent café has been opened in Union Square. Stephanie Tuder, writing in *Eater New York*, described its success, 'When it debuted in summer 2016, tourists stormed the place for bowls of cereal that are available at every bodega and grocery store throughout the country'. Maybe it's because pop-ups are *per se* more exciting, but the biggest lesson here is that a bit of theatre, a bit of chutzpah and a proper investment can pay off. There's plenty of life in that Kellogg's tiger given it has the stage on which to perform, and there's still plenty more to learn about consumers and their attitudes to breakfast.

Cass: pop-up and bringing art to more people

Cass art stores are emblazoned with the line, 'let's fill this town with artists'. Inside artists throng and non-artists who wish they were artists linger over expensive painting sets and cartridge paper wondering if they could create great art if only given the right materials.

Mark Cass started the business in the early 1980s. It now has 13 stores and turns over a little under £20 million. All the early stores were self-funded and nearly all the 190 staff are artists, which explains their enthusiasm. Mark latterly borrowed £3 million from the Business Growth Fund[1] to expand and develop an e-commerce strategy (this now produces 25 per cent of the company's turnover).

Professional management has been hired at the top of the business and they are now experimenting with pop-up stores, which cost a fraction of the £0.5 million it costs to stock and fit out a new store. These are in schools of art (Winchester was the first) and Selfridges for just 12 weeks. Pop-ups by nature of their spontaneity and intimacy seem a perfect way to stimulate the artistic appetites latent in so many people.

Pop-ups are like doodling, a great way to find out what sort of potential exists and, better still, they're an easy way of putting a scale-up toe in the water.

Mark's philosophy is this: 'Every child is an artist. The problem is how to remain an artist once we grow up'.

Pop-ups are like doodling, a great way to find out what sort of potential exists and, better still, they're an easy way of putting a scale-up toe in the water.

Small is beautiful and pop-ups prove it

Whenever we hear this we say, in agreeing, it is not necessarily true that 'scale saves money'. We both have very clear views about the best size of organization to create the most productive culture. We think 50 or less is the perfect size. (Reid Hoffman thinks it's 150 – that's the size when everyone knows everyone – but Reid is American, very rich and his brainchild LinkedIn now has 13,000 employees. Reid thinks bigger than we do.) Around 50 is when everyone knows what's going on, which leads in our experience to the best customer service. It's also a size in which a well-planted culture can bloom.

Culture is essential. It was Peter Drucker, the most respected management writer and guru, who has the saying, 'Culture eats strategy for breakfast' ascribed to him by, amongst others, the

Los Angeles Times in 2014. It's certainly true that however fine, apt and compelling a strategy may be, it can be sabotaged by a hostile culture. Great cultures are like those described by Brian Chesky, the founder of Airbnb. We've extracted the key points from a letter he sent to all Airbnb staff on Monday, 21 October 2013, entitled, 'Don't F*ck up the Culture':

> Culture is simply a shared way of doing something with passion... it is living the core values when you hire; when you write an email; when you are working on a project; when you are walking in the hall. We have the power, by living the values, to build the culture.

It sounds great, but it's really hard introducing this into a big company. It's easier to sustain it than create it. However, it's relatively easy to do it in a start-up, and it's axiomatic to the creation of a great pop-up. The reason we like pop-ups so much is that when a pop-up business is created as an adjunct to a larger business, ownership of it is transferred to the person running it, and the magic of culture creation and the passion to succeed emerge.

Do not regard the pop-up as just a fun experiment. All start-ups were pop-ups once and a pop-up can become a LinkedIn one day. Thinking about pop-ups is not to think about simple experiments. Sometimes a pop-up can enable the creator of it to realize they've started something new that potentially has a life of its own.

The pop-up approach in summary

It would be easy to think of pop-ups as rather small and amateurish. Certainly, they are a far cry from the concept of hairy, audacious goals and blitz scales as described by some US entrepreneurs specifically in the tech space. But the reality is few entrepreneurs have the financial resources to be that audacious. Having decided to start their own business was, in itself, a pretty audacious ambition.

The neat thing about pop-ups is they allow a business owner to get their hands dirty and their minds stimulated, whilst doing wonders for their powers of observation, all at low cost. In our experience too much time is spent on business plans and spreadsheets in an office rather than spending the time with real consumers watching, listening and empathizing with what they're feeling, when seeing, touching and trying your product.

We have often worked with very bright marketing people from, reputedly, the best and, certainly, the biggest companies who say they're too busy to get out into the street and see what real human beings are doing. If we stand in a supermarket and watch what people do, we'll be amazed that a lot of them really do read the labels and are fastidiously careful about what they buy.

But even better than standing in a supermarket is to create our own mini-shop or stall where we can really describe and illustrate what our idea is. Yes of course this is unrepresentative of the competitive reality of the crowded market, but, if with a captive market and our passionate enthusiasm we can't win over support, what chance does our poor product have out there on its own without its parent championing it?

Pop-ups can be more than a tactical device; they can be a way of revitalizing a languishing brand or a demotivated executive. They can be energizing and, sometimes, produce extraordinary results.

Here's a quote from the French author Antoine de Saint-Exupéry, which describes the difference between a left-brained approach to life and the right-brained, which embraces emotion, ambition and vision. It's the story potentially of a great story and successful pop-up:

If you want to build a ship,
don't drum up the people
to gather wood, divide the
work, and give orders.
Instead, teach them to yearn
for the vast and endless sea.

Note

1 Business Growth Fund is the most active investor in Britain and Ireland in growing businesses. As of December 2017, the company had invested £1.3 billion of its £2.5 billion balance sheet. They claim to be unobtrusive and empathetic in helping companies like Cass realize their ambitions, without taking control or exerting unhelpful pressure.

CHAPTER FIVE

Start-ups: How to do them. How to succeed

Preamble to a toolkit

Anyone starting a business, apart from having a clear understanding of what they're letting themselves in for, needs a toolkit that equips them to do all the basic stuff that makes a business work and seem solid. Here is that toolkit. With this, we will be able to get over the jumps safely on this start-up race course. Winning is something else. We'll come to that at the end.

First of all, good business is all about planning. In 1950, Dwight Eisenhower, one time US President and Commander in Chief of the Allied Army in the Second World War, wrote a letter to a US diplomat in which he ascribed this remark to an unknown soldier:

> Plans are worthless. Planning is everything.

Just because we can produce beautiful, comprehensive business plans doesn't mean we can run a successful business unless, of course, it happens to be called 'Beautiful Business Plans Limited'.

It's the process of planning that equips us to deal with all contingencies. It's what we all do before we go on holiday – 'passport, money, credit cards, tickets, itinerary, insurance and so on'. We can always buy underwear, if we forget our pants, but a passport is more tricky. Planning is thinking within a logical framework. The planning process forces us to think of all the components in a business that, when synchronized properly, make it work.

It's about being prepared. Let's imagine you're running a business and someone comes along with an offer so stupendously large that you have to consider it very, very seriously. Every time you blink you see wads of imaginary banknotes. When they say they want to do due diligence, are you even close to being in a state where that is possible? Are your books and your historic data in good order? Could you answer any question thrown at you? If you can't, those wads of notes will evaporate.

It's about being consistent, about building a clear, sensible way to work once we've decided what we want our start-up business to be. More businesses fail because of bad management than because of a bad idea. Good execution is critical. Too few people are focused on the critical need to build a business machine that works. In today's world of six sigma (a proven method that provides organizations with tools to improve the capability of their business processes; it's been used with mathematical precision by GEC), consumers have been conditioned to expect zero defects. In the past, the AA and RAC did roaring business as cars kept on breaking down. Now this doesn't happen very often. The ability to create a business that day in, day out delivers a consistent, excellent product or service is even more important than a creative genius coming up with the very occasional great idea.

So what follows is our toolkit. It's important it's used well. Just because we have a chisel doesn't mean we can make a chair. But if we concentrate and read up an instruction manual at least we can get started.

Content

This is quite a long section so it may help you to show what's included.

PREPARATION – Getting in the right place mentally – the first steps

PLANNING – The 'Business Plan' – what to include, how to write it

BASICS – What you need to start a business (in simple terms)

MONEY – Getting money, managing money, allocating money

PERFORMANCE – Finding advisers and managing the business

THINKING – How you think and how to find the style that suits the business

PEOPLE – How to hire, manage and coach people

CUSTOMERS – How to plan marketing and sales, especially how to serve customers

BEYOND START-UP – Finding the options. Thinking of growth. Managing scaling-up

A SUCCESS STORY – Rachel Bell's story. Lessons to learn

Snapshot lessons from recent start-up people

We asked some people doing a start-up or close to starting-up, to give us some simple advice on the good things they've done or seen done; the things that should have been done and either weren't done or weren't done enough and the biggest lesson from starting a business.

Monika Radclyffe: Incubator Director, SETsquared Bristol

GOOD THINGS
Have an end point in mind.

SHOULD DO'S

Don't go it alone. Get a co-founder. Build a network of advisers around you.

Don't think obsessively about the product. Think about how you're going to sell it first.

Build a board early.

BIGGEST LESSONS

Make a plan; set deadlines for yourself (how long can you afford not to pay yourself?).

And join an incubator.

Dr Becky Sage: CEO, Interactive Scientific

GOOD THINGS

Have resilience and patience. (And when on the verge of running out of money, explore every last avenue…don't give up.)

SHOULD DO'S

Listen harder to the little voice inside your head if it says, 'this is not working; this is not ok'.

Delegate more and expect more from others.

Focus on your market until confident that there's a place in it for your product.

Build more strong, valuable relationships in all parts of the business.

BIGGEST LESSONS

Get the right people around you and find ways to value your own self-worth.

Merlie Calvert: business start-up, lawyer and mentor

GOOD THINGS
Start with values – and a sense of mission that's far bigger than just one or two individuals.

SHOULD DO'S
Start sooner. Be braver.

BIGGEST LESSONS
Be a magnet. Build a strong network of great people before you need to ask for help. Commercial paralysis or giving up happens when you don't know how to do stuff that matters.

Whenever you get stuck, someone will know the right answer, or be able to connect you with someone else who does.

Al Taylor: ex McKinsey; serial (successful) entrepreneur

GOOD THINGS
Don't be tempted to scale before you are ready, otherwise you'll just waste money.

SHOULD DO'S
Mostly I wished we'd used marketing hacks. They understand search engine optimization and how to make your money work. They 'get' digital marketing algebra. We (mostly) don't.

BIGGEST LESSONS
The most important thing is the business model. The best entrepreneurs in the world can't make a bad business model successful.

Delay taking money from investors as long as you can. This allows you more time to refine the model so you have confidence that it will work (as well as giving you more leverage).

Preparation

Getting ourselves into the right frame of mind

We hear a lot of people talking about skillsets and competence, about data, analysis and insights. And these are very important. A talent package that we need in business. As American Express used to say in their advertising, 'don't leave home without it'. But there are some other things we need even more – self-belief, a positive attitude and a sense of purpose.

Being stressed – as so many people are nowadays – is not the right mindset to have when starting anything, let alone a new business. If we are stressed working for our big, fat corporation where everyone is told what to do, we can coast along. But when we're running our own business we need to be on our toes, and those toes had better not be shaking with terror. Instead, you need to be in a state of coiled relaxation like a powerful spring.

How do we achieve this blessed state?

Give yourself space to think and to listen

So much of our working lives is a mix of being driven to complete other people's delegated work, being trapped in meetings where we have little to offer, and even less interest, or we're doing work we think is unimportant, leads nowhere or alternatively leads to places we believe are just plain wrong.

To be a successful start-up we need to get out of the confines of a big office building, breathe some fresh air and think; think without a spreadsheet or computer screen, just plain, old-fashioned pondering. Before we go to sleep, we should think about our key tasks for the next day. Thinking about how we'll crack the problem that's been vexing us often gets that problem solved in our brains whilst we sleep. We should prepare for our working life by creating a get-away from it 'think time' every day.

We should talk to wise, calm friends about ideas and options when we're going through those pre-birth pains of starting a new business. We all have a few such counsellors. They could be an uncle, father-in-law, grandparent, next door neighbour – someone who has either seen it all or has that special capacity to get to the nub of a problem. Someone who says something like, 'Have you thought of saying, "this is wrong because of the following"…as opposed to going along with something that you know is going to go wrong?'

The sort of advice a grown-up, of whom there are quite a few around, can give us. When listening to advice, really concentrate and really listen – it's called 'active listening' – it's something we seldom do.

Keep the juices flowing

That's easier said than done. Telling people to change mood is like asking them to be happy, and it's thoroughly unhelpful. You can't just be something like that, to order. But inspiration (literally, breathing in ideas) depends on external stimulation from books, films, conversation, sunsets, music or anything that triggers energy in us. Let's think hard about those things that refuel our enthusiasm. Increasingly, as we become busier running our own business, we'll need such boosts. We need to decide what works for us, when we need to play a certain piece of music, call a special mentor, or simply go out and have a conversation with some friends.

Invest, don't spend

Increasingly, we need to think about money. Money in any new business is a key concern. Daniel Ross, himself a seasoned investor in new businesses, has a clearer view than most about money. He's worked at Barclays Wealth, Crowd Bank, where he was Head of Sales and Investor Relations, and is now the UK Head of Yellowwoods Venture Investments. He is very terse about the casual way some start-ups waste money. 'Money', he snaps, 'often runs out needlessly.' Clearly what it takes for a start-up to be successful is very different from what it takes to be a successful, salaried employee with easy access to overdrafts. What start-up wannabees need to become are *Scrooges*. It requires a whole new fiscal mindset, and many of us find that very uncomfortable.

Find the good idea that you believe in

Whether we're about to start a business because we want to be free of corporate bureaucracy, or because we, and some colleagues, think there must be a better way of living our lives, or because we're out of work and 'resting', which is just not our thing, we need an idea, a proposition and a plan.

But first of all, we need that idea. Something that we believe we can sell to other people.

One immediate word of advice we should all heed. Generally, we should stick to our knitting; focus on what we know, on what our skills are. In short we should play to our strengths. But of course skills can be transferable and we, with marketing skills, could join a chef and a restaurateur in creating a new restaurant. What we must do is reflect on our limitations, our strengths and our passions.

For instance, we shouldn't plan to start a vegan restaurant if we're not vegetarian let alone vegan, have never run a restaurant or anything like a restaurant, and hate being in front-line service. Recipes for disaster accompany such journeys into the unknown.

Two more words of advice:

- **It's better to aim at being better** at something than eccentrically original. Too many people want to be unique when it would be far better to be better in quality, delivery and presentation on a more familiar product.

- **Don't try something you have no 'feel' for.** Why would we do that? Why would we, if we are not technologically adept, want to do a tech start-up? All businesses are not the same.

People with infinitely transferable skills are very unusual, despite what we may read in various management books. Starting a business is not a hobby. It's like a marriage or civil partnership. Liking, loving and wanting to spend time with our partner are indicative of being on the right track in terms of building a solid relationship. Starting a new business requires similar commitment and engagement. We need, critically, to look ahead and think of the future not just about the present or the immediate future. Do we think that we'll still like what we plan to initiate now in five years' time? If the answer's no, or maybe not, we should probably think again.

All our contacts, friends and friends of friends are potential customers

It's a subject of mystification, and of mirth, that so many people still persist in the almost 'mediaeval' pursuit of 'cold calling'. It's depressing to do it and even more depressing to be a recipient of it. But here's the real issue: it doesn't work.

If we want to start a business from scratch, we should give ourselves a break and talk to people who know something about us first. So our first action should be to put together a list of everyone we know, have met and with whom we've worked. LinkedIn will become our most important aid because it enables us to find out where people have been working and who knows who. It also allows us to join discussion groups, but that matters less than building up our network of people who know us.

Markets where there's an 'opening'

It's beginning to seem as though the Digitally Native Vertical Brand craze, as being the key to open up opportunities for new businesses, may have been rather overblown. Nonetheless, the principle of isolating opportunities in specific sectors that have ingrained consumer problems makes sense. These are markets that are lazy with sleepy brand leaders or duopolies (like the razor/razor blade market), markets that don't work efficiently or competitively (examples of this might include the legal profession or estate agencies), margin-fat markets (like mattresses, home furnishings and kitchenware) or markets with ingrained customer reluctance to changes (like utilities and banking).

All we need, as a new competitor in such a market, is the ability to deliver a better, cheaper, more efficient service and to generate enough noise to achieve cut-through. At first, all we need are some triallists and then, build awareness and a sense of momentum so as to achieve more widespread trial. 'All we need' is of course a mighty ask. Most people will settle for less lofty ambitions, but if you have the backing, track record and self-confidence, extraordinary things can happen. In his 2018 book *This is Marketing* Seth Godin says we should think small and build a team of loyal consumers who are our brand champions. Broadscale marketing can come later.

For instance, the vegetarian food market had been poorly served until 2018, but as trends towards greater consumption of vegetables started growing, things changed. If you put the insight about changing consumer behaviour and the supply deficit together, you end up with *Mixt Greens*, *All Green* or *Chloe* in the United States. More modestly in the UK, there are companies like the Petrides brothers' *Allplants,* which provides home delivery of frozen vegan ready meals and has expanded quickly since its 2017 launch in the UK.

Opportunities exist everywhere to create a new and exciting business. Only recently has the climate for experiment improved, with support from the media, funders, entrepreneurs and more adventurous consumers.

Values and missions

Philosophy and culture are words that have come to business quite recently. Until now, the MBAs have had it all their own mathematical way. But their business landscape has been invaded by poets, thinkers and philanthropists. Bill Gates, and his wife Melinda, have radically changed the way most of us think about 'doing good', but that desire to change the world, which they are fulfilling, has become widespread and growing. We use words like 'happy, fulfilled and relevant' a lot. If the third of our lives we spend at work isn't achieving those, then what on earth are we doing it for?

Ask why we get out of bed in the morning. It's an important question. Many years ago, Martin Conradi, on setting up the presentation business Showcase, said that every day was a new adventure. The biggest threat to the ability of big companies continuing to thrive will be that they are so boring. Their reasons for getting out of bed are money. That, and the protection of the machine in their charge that produces the money.

We can do better than that. Steve Jobs got it right – do we want to do something trivial or do we want to change the world? Or if not the world, how about our immediate circle, our town or, even, our country?

Our view is quite simple. Business, more often than not, is (or should be) the most entertaining and useful way to spend our time. It allows people, like us, to enjoy ourselves using our brains, our creativity and our skills to create something that other people find useful, helpful, interesting or amusing.

What better reason could there be to get up in the morning?

Why are we starting this business?

It helps at the outset if we're very clear why we are starting the business. Let's not fool ourselves. If it's to make lots of money, say so. There's nothing wrong with that. Neither is it wrong to do it to become famous or respected. But some of us will just do it for fun. When we stand outside a shop specializing in expensive stationery like Papersmith or nearly as expensive, Pen to Paper, we should rejoice in the fact that its creators wanted fun and self-satisfaction as well as financial success.

Becoming rich is not enough for most of us.

What are your main values in life?

In our helter-skelter modern world, little is certain. In 'chaos theory' there is something called 'the butterfly effect'. This effect means there's a causal link between a hurricane in China and a butterfly flapping its wings in New Mexico. It may take a very long time to come about, but the connection is real. If the butterfly had not flapped its wings at just the right point in space and time, the hurricane would not have happened. Chaos disrupts the rock-hard certainty of values. However, we believe if we don't have 'red-line' values we're in trouble as human beings. If we're struggling, we should ask which of the following matter most to us:

- **People** – for many of us it's the cut and thrust of conversation and the repartee of a high-performance business that inspires us most. In managing people, we find the most exciting thing is helping someone talented become a truly brilliant performer. All of this is, initially, likely to be missing in a start-up, but if that's what we need and want to feel truly fulfilled, we need to aim to create a business that employs people and, therefore, allows us to be what we really want – a great people manager and leader. And we can't do that if we create a highly profitable business but with few or no employees.

- **Things** – for some of us it would be the creation of a great shiny, state-of-the-art production plant that will thrill us, together with our Tesla Model S parked out at the front. This will be a high tech world where robots will replace people and artificial intelligence is a serious, overhead saving tool. This is the future. Zero defects. Zero staff.

- **Intellectual challenge** – for some, business is a game, a serious game like chess or bridge where the excitement is in solving the problem or in creating the 'perfect' case study. People like this tend to be consultants or MBAs who love change and complexity, who believe creating a successful business is almost reward enough in its own right.

- **Recognition** – particularly prevalent in ego-driven occupations like media, advertising, PR or politics, where the need for fame, publicity and recognition are pervasive. To be on the front page of *PRWeek* or *Campaign* was important and confidence building. To be called Shining Bell or Heavyweight Hall next to a moody picture of oneself was momentarily, we admit, thrilling and, presumably, still is for some of us.

- **Money** – in our research the motivation of money was surprisingly less important than it used to be, or than we'd expected it to be. Everyone is realistic in believing a business needs to be financially sound and successful in making consistent and sustainable profits. Alternatively, success may come from creating the momentum that allows a company to achieve high market capitalizations. A US company called Lyft (a rival to Uber) generated a turnover of US $2.2 billion, losses of US $970 million, yet was valued at US $15 billion in 2019.

Our desire for money may affect our behaviour and management style. But many people in today's world are not sure this is a price worth paying. Admitting to and embracing our values is a personal thing. The very worst thing we can do is to fudge them. If we want to make lots of money quickly, we shouldn't try to be a 'touchy-feely' people manager too. The two are irreconcilable.

But if we want to build a great business, short-term profit is not the key thing.

That killer proposition

We've got to find that short, brilliant, killer proposition for the business. People get paid a lot of money in advertising for their ability to create concise slogans. The reason why it's so important to have a short snappy proposition, is the discipline it imposes. Too often in creative briefs we've seen someone trying to appeal to everyone and say everything there is to say about a product. To do this in the real world and expect it to have any effect on human consumers, is a futile ambition. Like trying to shoot down a plane with a shotgun. Big bang, lots of pellets, zero impact.

We need one or two sentences that say what makes us stand out and imply why people should buy our offering. About 25 words should do it. It needs to be honest, truthful, arresting and address what people want. One of the most important words in creating such a proposition is 'BECAUSE'… because it is the link to evidence and not puffery. An example:

> This book should help you succeed in creating a start-up business **because** it is written by two people who understand from experience how to succeed.

So we must decide our 'because' points and we'll have the makings of our proposition. The biggest problem is in keeping it short. Here's what Mark Twain said in reflecting on the difficulty of being concise:

> I didn't have time to write a short letter, so I wrote a long one instead. (In a letter from Mark Twain to James Redpath, Elmira, New York. 15 June 1871)

Planning

Producing a start-up plan

Who's this start-up plan meant for? If this is a tool for extracting funding, this should be reflected with every word and figure we write. If it's for the bank and other stakeholders, being comprehensive, confident and well-presented still matters. If it's just for us and our partner(s) as a landmark reference, we should still take care in its preparation because this is a manifesto about us and our future.

Decide who it's for before you do anything else.

EXECUTIVE SUMMARY

This is what we'll craft last of all when we're in a position to summarize properly. But here are some tips. Try to keep the summary reduced to just five or six key points. These could be five or six '**because**' points. Here's a simple example of what they might look like. Each point obviously needs to be amplified and given real substance:

- Because the idea's strong enough to cut through and engages consumers in a noisy world.

- Because there's a significant and quantifiable market opportunity.

- Because the start-up principals and team are well qualified to exploit that opportunity.

- Because research shows the proposition will be very well accepted by our target market.

- Because the financial projections look exciting as well as being realistic, short and medium term.

- Because the business planning is thorough and well thought through.

Finally, if funding is being sought, an exit plan within five or fewer years will need to be included.

THE SALES PROPOSITION

The short, brilliant, killer proposition for the business (see above). We shouldn't be proud (or foolish) but instead get a professional copywriter to help. These are the most important 25 or so words in the plan, and possibly our life.

THE OPPORTUNITY

It's time for realism and pragmatism. Everyone starts as a sceptic when they're presented with a new idea, and their 'what's wrong with it or what could go wrong?' antennae are on full alert.

Now's the time to explain how and where we spotted the opportunity that we're describing. We should also demonstrate the forensic process involved (a little post rationalization is allowed).

Any investor will want to know about the cost of entry for us (and any other potential competitor). How much, how long and what will it take for competitors to destroy us? How much will it cost to scale the concept? What (realistically) do we believe the growth trajectory would look like and over what period? Why do we believe that and what would it take to significantly accelerate the growth? It may be that the growth will be slow but solid and of little interest to an ambitious investor but good enough for us who are self-funding (bootstrapping) the business.

We should consider the need for capital investment, for marketing investment and the people we'll need to accelerate our speed to market. We also need to be clear on how we'll build reliable logistics and, critically, how we can realize the opportunity at the lowest possible cost. There will be options and decisions about alternatives here. We should outline and consider them with our preferred option.

Do not overpromise. Justify assertions and claims. Include evidence to prove the story is well thought through and not a fantasy.

MARKET ANALYSIS

Here's the opportunity to show that we're thorough and that we really know what we're talking about.

How big is the market in volume and value? What are the trends? Have there been any anomalies or key moments of disruption when the structure of the market has changed? Who are the main competitors and what has been the recent change in share and competitive activity?

Has any useful consumer research been accessed? We'll have conducted and include the key findings of our 'thumbnail research' – that's our phrase for getting friends, peers and expert marketeers we may know who are in the target market round to talk about the issues they see in the market. We'll include interviews with journalists and well-informed writers on the subject. We'll also include any relevant news articles with comments from us.

Depending on the market, we'll have done store visits, talked to trade customers and got a sense of how the market dynamics work and the current particular issues. If this is an online market, it should be relatively easy via LinkedIn or media contacts to get a good feel for issues, changes and market gaps.

The challenge is to seem professional, thorough, *deeply* inquisitive and astute as to how change is affecting the status and future potential for the market.

OUTLINE MARKETING PLAN

This is covered in more detail later in this section. It's important to show that we aren't going to spend huge sums on marketing and that we have a very keen eye on the return on investment. There are five key questions:

- *Who is our target market* – no waffle about secondary targets – precisely who, broken down by demographics and psychographics, are our 'bullseye consumers'?
- *Why should they buy our product or service* and, if switching from another brand, which one and why will that be?
- *How will we achieve our key launch need,* which will usually be maximizing awareness and interest within our target market?
- *How much money do we need* to achieve our objectives?
- *What are the key activities* on which we plan to focus?

Clarity is what most marketing plans lack. We must be clear, straightforward and simple.

MANAGEMENT TEAM

Any funder or stakeholder will want to know about our own credentials, experience, skills and views. Why are we embarking on this adventure? It had better sound good and plausible. In our experience, people's CVs are historical lists rather than self-perceptive stories about a human being equipping themselves for the next adventure. But they shouldn't be a sales pitch either.

Our partner or partners are critical. Why are we partners? 'I've known Jim all my life' or 'we're best friends' are not persuasive reasons. This isn't a club; it's a business we're starting. We should be focusing on how the skills we have intermesh and why there's a synergy of attitude in our partnership. Most of all is there 'team fit'? Increasingly, people are looking for alliances and partnerships that are stable and complementary. If we can't convincingly describe this, maybe the partnership itself isn't all that it should be.

FINANCIALS

This section must be solid, clear and convincing. Everyone knows that even with the best will and skill in the world, any financial plan will tend to be wrong. We'll either undershoot or exceed it and for perfectly legitimate reasons. What we have to demonstrate is that the process by which we produce our financial plan shows we have a complete understanding and grasp of the levers that operate the business and that we're controlling. A perfect, complimentary comment about the financials from an expert outsider would be that they are 'clear and competent'.

We should ensure this section is brief, salient and that all the key numbers are highlighted. There may be a lot of numbers. If so, we'll put the bulk of them in the appendices. This plan we're writing is a story, and stories benefit from selective detail. We'll also find it helpful to show plans at a series of levels so that the relative sensitivities can be seen.

Plan A – realistic, cautious; Plan B – a 'stretch' plan that assumes certain specified things go right; and Plan C – a target 'exit plan' that shows how, if it comes to an exit, levers can be pulled to maximize short-term sales and profit.

A word on the 'exit strategy' . Earlier in *Start-ups, Pivots and Pop-ups* we said we deplored the overuse of the 'exit' word. We did so on the basis that we should not, for preference, be looking to make a fast buck but instead a sustainable cash-generative business. But if we're looking to secure funding, we have to be realistic about funders' motives. They want to know, should they be in a position to persuade us to exit, what the value of the business, given a cash injection, could be worth in three to five years.

The words that go with the numbers will be really important in demonstrating our command of those numbers and their sensitivity and our competence (that word again).

FUNDING NEEDS

We need to decide whether we require funds to make our start-up succeed. In service businesses like advertising and PR, it's often possible to self-fund the business and avoid having a rapacious, inquisitive or unlikeable stakeholder. But the general view is that having seed-money may prevent us making bad decisions just to generate short-term sales. Reid Hoffman says it's essential to have a series of fundraisings to allow our ambitions to be realized. If we have a great idea, we need to feed it. But bear in mind he's very tech focused.

The questions are these:

- How much money are we putting in?
- What do we need the money for?
- How much difference will it make?
- If we can't raise funds, will our start-up collapse?

So this section will only exist at all if our business plan is also a pitch for funding.

WHAT'S NEXT?

This is where the more speculative nature of forecasting our future can be addressed. In our experience there's a 'what now?' moment about a year after a start-up. We've put away our short trousers and are going to 'big school'. We're no longer 'news'. This is not a project; it's a business and businesses need to know where they are trying to go. Including a set of scenarios and questions that need to be asked and answered should come here. This section needs to be written for our own personal consumption, or if we're raising funds, written circumspectly.

CONCLUSION

Our opportunity to express rousingly the essential reason that this business can, should and deserves to be a success.

APPENDICES

In our experience this will be the longest bit of the plan. It will contain a lot of numbers, research reports and detailed CVs. Having this receptacle for all the evidence allows the main part of the plan to be easier to read and the arguments in it clearer.

OVERALL COMMENTS

The quality of the presentation, the layout and the clarity of the indexing are essential. People are busy and overloaded with data, often too dense to absorb easily and usually laid out in a dull, unreadable way. Interestingly, Fast Company has research that shows CEOs are amongst the most voracious consumers of books, reading on average over a book a week (60 a year in fact). Publishers of books are experts at knowing how to make words easy to absorb, so we should make our business plan like the first few pages of a book.

It's money well spent getting a freelance art director to make the plan look professional. DIY is not such a great idea especially when the recipients of this plan already see so many such documents.

The basics

Here briefly are some of the things we have to plan, and do, if we're starting a business. There's no rocket science here, just a list of prosaic stuff that needs to be done.

Our identity

We think too many people spend too much time worrying about their name and their identity. A great name and logo won't make for a great start-up, neither will a bad one stop you succeeding. Who would ever have thought Helena Rubinstein would be a great name for a cosmetic company?

Some people have playful names – Shine, John Doe, Mischief; other names are more serious sounding – French Gold Abbott, FCO, Hall Triggle Rosner Parker. So long as we're comfortable, happy or, hopefully, thrilled, that's enough. We just need to be proud to say who we are. Generally, name generation has become a nightmare, particularly if we want to be unique, because computers seize hold of most names now. Good names are shamelessly stolen. Just see how many 'Shines' there are now.

More importantly the look and logo design matter because they set the tone of what we stand for. We need a good, intelligent and skilled designer or art director to create this. It's a quick and painless process if we talk together so each gets to understand the other. In a DIY digital world, where Apple can make a bad idea look almost OK, we may be tempted to do our own. Don't. We don't do our own dentistry do we? This is much more important.

The basic stuff

WHO ARE WE?
We need cards and that identity on a letterhead that appears on all the basic collateral we need – invoices, terms of business, email footers, etc.

WHERE ARE WE?
We need a registered business address (usually our accountant) plus a work address, a registered business number and (if applicable) a VAT number. We need to establish our existence. We need to be on LinkedIn for sure (but as regards other social media, we can decide on what suits us). We are personally

agnostic about this, believing far too much time is spent worrying about social media with much of it just time consuming and unproductive.

WHAT ARE WE?

We can establish this quickly and professionally on LinkedIn, which we can actually do ourselves with a personal and a business posting. We need a website if we want to be taken seriously.

These are relatively easy to produce, but it's far better to get a professional to produce something simple, stylish and low-cost to begin with. Most of all, be informative. People visiting your site will not pore over it, so make the following information hit them fast:

- what you do;
- your point of difference;
- what you stand for;
- who you are;
- what you've done;
- what people say about you;
- where you are and how to reach you.

WHAT DO WE HAVE TO SAY TO PROSPECTIVE CUSTOMERS?

We need to create a sales pitch that's updated quarterly. It will probably be most useful as a brief PowerPoint presentation of, say, no more than 10 slides that should be designed as a conversation-provoker. We should be agile enough to modify our pitch to the circumstances and the needs of individual customers.

Presentation coaching may be the best investment we can make in the early days of a start-up.

We should never underestimate the need to become a confident and fluent presenter. We'll be doing a lot of presentations and the way we do them will directly correlate to our sales success. Presentation coaching may be the best investment we can make in the early days of a start-up.

HOW DO WE GET PAID?

This is a critical issue. When in a big company (if we were), this was someone else's job. Not any longer. Not being paid on time is like being starved of oxygen. We also need to be assiduous about paying bills on time as well as being paid ourselves. People love being paid promptly. Having a reputation of being a good payer is worth having.

We'll have comprehensive, up-to-date terms of business (from our accountant, a company like Farillio or the CFO of any friendly company giving us a template). Stuff like this sounds boringly bureaucratic, but we have to pay attention to it.

Getting started...the key steps

Here are some of the things we need to do in the first month or so.

IMPRESSIONS

1 We are not in a fashion show, but too many start-up people look scruffy, as though rebelling against their corporate past. Don't be like that. Looking smart says you are ambitiously in control.

2 Be observant and listen hard because we need to be aware of what's going on in the market, in the news and in trends. We should be soaking up information and insights and not be shy about asking people for their advice.

3 We need to enjoy the buzz of being our own boss and look confident and energetic.

4 In these early days we are making important first and what will be long-lasting impressions.

LAUNCHING THE BUSINESS

Because it's much easier making a noise at the beginning when our story is news, we should take advantage of this. Focus on just a few publications or channels. Aim to get a decent article or radio interview with which we can merchandise via our website or via email to key contacts. We should use the news value of our launch as vigorously as we can. The media interest will wane fast unless we have something new to say. We'll avoid big parties and boozy lunches because we can't afford them, and in current times they send off inappropriate signals. It's also worth getting a professional PR business to help you on your way. Why reinvent the wheel when, for very little, you can have a Formula 1 team to help?

In our experience it's better to have a great relationship with one or two journalists who understand what you are doing. Empathy is our most useful tool. Working out what they want, not what we want is the key. We need to have stories to tell, not products to sell. Any self-respecting writer or journalist hates being used as a device for anyone to advertise their wares. And they're right.

SAMPLING AND FEEDBACK

Whatever the product, be it a pork pie or an app, the most important thing to do is to get people to try it. Whether we use a pop-up or something less elaborate, our key task in the early days is to get people to try, comment and, if they like it, be persuaded to endorse it and spread the word.

If it's a new bike, we should give a few away to the most famous or well-connected people we know and take photographs of them riding. If it's a vegan ready meal, get non-vegans to try and hopefully say 'this is absolutely delicious – amazing'. The key is to get trial and news. At railway stations, in office blocks, in wine bars. The biggest challenge is to collect data about real people trying a real product and saying honestly what they think. The feedback is as important as the sampling.

HAVING SOMEWHERE TO WORK FROM

The way we work nowadays has changed radically. Historically, the more senior we were the more likely we were to be imprisoned in a large walnut-panelled office with a PA outside in a large office too. But the modern CEO and senior executive is, three weeks in four, out on the road seeing customers, talking to and coaching the people who are working for them. If they're a listed business their lives revolve around quarterly reporting, so they think in 12-week cycles.

The trophy gleaming headquarters is becoming increasingly redundant as an office block. Diageo's HQ in Park Royal, West London, is a live poster site, shop and museum with tiny hot-desking work cubicles, seldom used, and some big meeting rooms. Global business executives travel. They don't hide in offices.

New businesses are no different. If we aren't travelling around, talking, pitching, learning then we aren't in business.

But we do need a base. Not a Starbucks or home. We need an inspiring location that makes us feel great whenever we go there. This is what WeWork wanted to create, and here's how they describe their culture in their 2019 Global Impact Report:

> Culture provides the momentum and interpersonal connection that can make your company a place where people want to pour themselves into work that they're passionate about.

Co-working spaces are getting better, more modern and more stylish. We should look around and see if we can find one that thrills us and is a great base for the few hours a week that we'll be there. And, remember, people will trust us more if they know we're a proper business with a proper address.

Money

Investment pays off

Money is the root of all development. The most striking thing about London, Mumbai, Shanghai or Seattle, or any successful city, is the amount of money it takes to create change. Just 50 years ago, London still bore the scars of war, but today, thanks to the billions spent on infrastructure investment, it has one of the most exciting skylines in the world and some of the most thrilling pieces of architecture.

GETTING FUNDS

There are a series of ways to raise money, although, according to The British Bank Report, despite the increased activity amongst women entrepreneurs the difficulty women have in raising funds remains sadly acute. As one anonymous female source said:

> We all know we don't get money; we all know it takes time to build a business, we all know women invest less and we all know there is not enough gender equality.

And we all know this anthem of despair will, on the basis of current trends, pretty soon – hopefully – be out of date as well as out of place.

Currently the most obvious sources for money are:

Bootstrapping Self-funding is safe, sensible and slow. A business like PR or marketing services can cope with small start-up funds. One that depends on R&D, or needs capital investment, cannot.

Angel funds An angel investor is an affluent individual, often a successful entrepreneur or business person, who provides capital for a business start-up, usually in exchange for convertible debt or ownership equity.

Their motives are not just monetary but because they also enjoy the thrill of advising and helping start-ups. Organizations like The Angel Investment Network give more information.

Banks Since the banking crisis of 2008, banks have been decreasingly helpful as sources of funding. Scandals like the massive fraud perpetrated by some rogue bankers and their consultant friends at its HBOS unit against small businesses unit in the Thames Valley region between 2002 and 2007 have made that situation worse. Whilst it's recognized that start-ups are migrating from big banks to other sources, our suspicion is that the banks will change. Coutts, for example, has started a very active programme of helping start-ups.

Family funds Funds like Daniel Ross's Yellowwoods Venture Investments, Omidyar and Kapor are all active in start-up funding. They are tax-efficient vehicles for families and can be helpful to start-ups.

VCs Venture capital, also called VC, refers to the financing of a start-up company by typically high-wealth investors who think the business has potential to grow substantially in the long run. They are the same in concept as an angel investor but usually handling very much larger sums of several million pounds.

Funding Circle and others Funding Circle is a peer-to-peer lending marketplace allowing investors to lend money directly to small- and medium-sized businesses. Funding Circle was the first website to use the process of peer-to-peer lending for business funding in the UK, and it is now the UK's largest marketplace lender to businesses. It had a rather disappointing IPO in 2018 but is nonetheless valued at over £1 billion – pretty good after just eight years' trading.

Government-backed funds Government-backed start-up loans of £500 to £25,000 are available to start or grow businesses. Unlike a business loan, this is an unsecured personal loan. We get free support and guidance to help write our business plan, and if successful we get up to 12 months of free mentoring.

CHOOSING THE RIGHT FUNDING PARTNER
Raising money may seem a headache and can take a long time. The issue is not just about raising money, it's about choosing the

right partner. In general terms, whatever the terms offered, we should never borrow money from people whom we don't respect, trust and like. The contribution a good partner can make goes way beyond money. We should think of them as a partner, not just as a source of money. We are, then, in it together with them and see them as an experienced and sympathetic member of our team.

Cash flow (next to sales it's the most important thing)

Are we being boring? If the definition of a bore is someone who goes on and on saying the same thing, then yes we are. Cash is king. Not generating it and not having it in the bank leads to problems. We need to have a professional helping to look after the money. We tend to expect income to turn into cash faster than it usually does and for costs to fall due later than they usually do. The consequence is a cash flow crisis, often explained away as a 'timing anomaly'.

Nearly all the problems we have in life spring from what Daniel Kahneman called 'pervasive optimistic bias'. This bias generates the illusion of control, that we have substantial control of our lives. What he calls the 'planning fallacy' is the tendency to overestimate benefits and underestimate costs, impelling people to take on risky projects.

He explains that humans fail to take into account complexity and that their understanding of the world consists of a small and, inevitably, unrepresentative set of observations. Furthermore, the mind generally does not account for the role of chance and therefore falsely assumes that a future event will mirror a past event.

'Cash flow projections' need to assume that not everything goes to plan. Any cash flow plan that doesn't include a contingency provision for delays in payment is not very useful. It's sensible to have a sum of money held in reserve to deal with the unexpected.

Financial management/advice/help

This is where we must, repeat must, get the best advice and support we can find and afford. Getting the best, most useful advice is absolutely key to our succeeding. We need an experienced financial eye helping plan our cash flow, our capital investment needs, our margins (and how to improve them) and monthly management accounts.

The real key is to know where we are, where things are heading and to avoid surprises. We need a map-maker, a navigator and a look-out. Expressed like that, the finance guru becomes a lot less esoteric and a lot more of a life-saver.

For those of us who are spenders rather than savers, leading a start-up can prove a rather rude shock. We must become a saver of the small sums; the culture we create must be spartan rather than indulgent. Aldi rather than Waitrose. We need every penny to keep the business afloat and help it grow.

We shall also need advice on how, legally, to minimize tax, to get our VAT done safely, to set up the insurance we need and how to purchase the basics for our business life: mobile phone, laptop, basic apps like QuickBooks, or whatever is recommended, and on what terms.

A good financial adviser will ask us lots of questions. The aim is to make our business safer, smoother and easier to run.

Performance

We have to measure how we are doing

We've consistently said that DIY should be avoided when it comes to specialist areas like tax, legal stuff and design. We are starting a business. All our waking time should be spent on sales, production, quality control and customer service. We need to focus and avoid being distracted by doing stuff we might actually do quite well but which takes our attention away from the main game.

We are the team strikers: so let's stop working on the turnstiles. But obviously, as a start-up, we're pragmatists – sometimes we have to do things that we'd rather not because we can only employ those whom we can afford. Let's choose the best we can afford and people who are recommended by people we know.

And remember, these are all, hopefully, long-term partnerships not quick transactions. For our part we should be pitching our business to them, so they can understand its potential and our commitment to it. All the big London firms tend to be expensive, for legitimate reasons, but let's bear in mind there's a real caché in working with start-ups that prove to be a real success. Working with recently formed winners is intoxicating for big, successful (and possibly bored) big company executives who probably envy us.

Finding the right specialist advisers is vital

LAWYER

The biggest nightmare is to face a legal action that could have been avoided if we'd spent the time and money getting contracts drawn up properly in the first place. We'll need Articles of Association, shareholders' agreements, employee contracts (ready to use when we start hiring people), supplier contracts, terms of business and rental agreements if we are renting an office or anything else. These are easy for a lawyer and a sheer waste of our time. We'd choose a local lawyer we liked and whose credentials are endorsed by people we respect and agree the best terms we could. If they can't understand we're a poor, needy start-up, we shouldn't work with them. Besides which, we've hopefully sold them on our plan and vision. Lawyers serve two purposes. They do all that contractual stuff that's essential and they act as confidantes and bodyguards when something unexpected turns up.

ACCOUNTANT

We should trust that our accountants protect us and ensure we don't pay more tax than we should. They will probably be local, which saves time, and will be able to give us good advice on a wide series of subjects. If they're local to our business, they will also have a lot of potentially useful contacts.

FINANCIAL/ADMINISTRATIVE ADVISER

In our research amongst start-ups, one of the biggest regrets that owners have expressed is that, with hindsight, one of the first things they should have done is to have found an energetic, creative, experienced financial person to help them. The biggest help they may provide is to help solve the dilemma of when, at a given moment, an injection of cash could make a big difference. Their experience would be critical. A lot of very good retired finance directors or financial advisers, who've set up their own consultancies, are available to help. The same 'health warning' applies as before. Do we like and respect them, and are their credentials right for what we need?

MARKETING/PR/DESIGN ADVISERS

Some of the brightest and most experienced business people appoint lawyers, accountants and HR professionals to help them but believe they can do their own advertising, press releases and packaging design. Is this because years of pent-up frustration with bad advertising or PR agencies, when we worked for a big company, have made us cynical? Mark Riley, ex London ad man who has his own business, Riley Communications in Suffolk, in part blames Apple, which can help make a terrible idea look quite smart, slick and shiny. Mark is just one of the most remarkable semi-retired talents out there doing better work than when they worked in London and were earning a lot of money. The key thing is they're doing it now for more modest sums because they love it.

Advice: We should not do our own operations: we should employ a surgeon.

Having said this we should take our time, listen to recommendations, look at the work they've done and have a lot of conversations about their experience with small, start-up businesses. We should try working with them on a trial basis before appointing them permanently, but when we decide to appoint them we should make this a proper contractual relationship *because we'll need a real partnership with people who make us look good, as we grow.*

MENTOR

The other source of regret we hear is from people who failed to work with an experienced mentor. Starting our own business will be at best a bit stressful, at worst a nightmare. If we were to ask Sir Martin Sorrell or Lord Saatchi what their early months and years at WPP or Saatchi & Saatchi were really like, they'd go pale at the recollection. They were both white-knuckle, roller-coaster experiences. So we should spend a long time finding someone who's kind, experienced, uplifting and helpful. Their job is to bring out the best in us. *A good mentor can be the biggest aid to productivity we'll find.*

IT SERVICING EXPERT

A good day can suddenly become a rotten one if there's an IT failure. Let's be sure, whatever else, that we get a good, practical reliable 24/7 IT expert to calm our nerves and solve our problems. Beware being so reliant on technology that you forget how to function if something goes wrong. Dave Trott , founder of several advertising agencies including Gold Greenlees Trott, said this, 'A blind belief in technology is the Achilles heel of the lazy'.

Fortunately, good IT guys exist and they're essential for our sanity.

Using technology should save time and money

If you're under 40, this whole section is irrelevant. You know so much more than we do. If you're over 50, you'll be saying 'thank heavens'.

In the 21st century, we have acquired a rather strange relationship with technology. The young have known nothing else and for them it's as easy as riding a bicycle. Issues of privacy simply don't seem to bother them. If they're middle-aged, they've learnt to crack it but are a little nervous of some of the privacy issues and frustrated their young children are more skilled than they are. If they're older, there are some who wish it would go away and are terrified of invasions of privacy. For others, the internet is a gateway to a new world.

But the fact is, we'll run any business better if we embrace the best of technology. Emails speed things up, GPS stops us getting lost, Wikipedia informs us (but let's be careful to double-check facts), the web allows us to know more, to know more widely, to get information quickly and to research competition and new opportunities. It does nearly everything we could wish from a PA, except for the most important thing of all: it doesn't think.

So let's not be luddites. Let's embrace the good stuff but never allow it to become a time waster. What we need are a few rules:

1 Do not keep mobile phones on or in view in meetings, at lunch or in 1-2-1 conversations.

2 Have a 'simplicity strategy'. Don't be persuaded to have state-of-the-art gear as that's usually a mistake. Regard technology like shoes. Comfort is more important than novelty.

3 On the other hand, it probably looks a bit eccentric to be using an old Nokia.

4 We are in charge. We should not allow any piece of technology to bully us.

5 In general, we should be wary of social media. Its value as an advertising medium has been widely traduced by Mark Ritson, a professor of marketing and a writer. Beware the amount of time that can be wasted on Facebook or Twitter. Most smart people are becoming more circumspect about social media nowadays.

6   We should assess the ROI of our spend on IT or get someone to do that for us. It's easy to spend on technology what we wouldn't spend on something else that might actually produce better sales results.

Low-cost, continuous research keeps you close to your customers

We are great believers in keeping as close to our market as we can. Too many new wave marketeers and business owners are trapped in front of their PCs or phones when they ought to be out of their office listening to their consumers and the drumbeat of the marketplace.

FOCUS GROUPS

There are some good, trained psychologists who do excellent quantitative research. But in a start-up situation we almost certainly can't afford the sort of money they charge. What we believe in is getting a group of people – friends or friends of friends – talking to us over a bottle of wine or coffee to help in finding, not just the truth (that they never tell us as David Ogilvy reminded us) but some consumer language and attitudes and where they place our product within their own hierarchy of importance. *We will very seldom waste our time by listening to potential consumers.*

STORE TRIPS

Nothing beats wandering along a high street, market or shopping centre to see some of the new things that are going on. Rather than just doing your shopping, go round a big Tesco and see what's new or surprising on the shelves. Ask why the displays of Heinz Tomato Ketchup have been radically reduced and the displays of vegetarian ready meals have been radically increased. Look at what's new in household cleaners and biscuits (have you noticed the vast array of Scandinavian savoury biscuits?).

These brief, frequent trips are brain-food, inspiring us to look, listen and think.

POP-UPS SHOW CONSUMERS IN CLOSE-UP

We've talked about these at some length, but the value of placing products in a competitive environment, including on their own or with competitive brands, will teach us a lot. This can be in a market, in a local community site like a church or church hall, as a concession in a store, or in a big pub at a weekend. We should think of our target market and choose our site accordingly. Context matters, so let's try to pop up where people who'll be most likely to want our product will hang out.

ROUNDTABLES

These are rather more sophisticated affairs designed to provoke deep thought. This requires the help of a few people who have useful contacts. Assemble a couple of journalists, a couple of business authors, a couple of retailers, a couple of CEOs/CMOs (Chief Marketing Officers), a couple of consultants and a couple of smart individuals – maybe an entrepreneur and a retired banker. Have an agenda of broad-ranging questions and spend two hours debating and collectively thinking about them. (What's needed is a mix of articulate bright people; there's no need to be too prescriptive about their occupations.) To succeed, we'll need a practised chairperson.

This will give us at the very least good material for a thought leadership piece, and it would be surprising and disappointing if we didn't get some useful insights too.

Measurement of key performance indicators

It's easy to be so busy that we don't have time to measure how we're doing. That's rather like being in such a hurry that we can't check how much petrol we have in the tank of the car. There's a commercial for Gordon's Gin (made by ad agency

Anomaly in 2018) where two girls, Kate and Hannah, are on the phone. One asks the other how busy she is:

'How busy? Just incredibly busy, the busiest of the busy that's how busy I am.'

'Oh. Too busy for a 5pm G&T then?'

'No, obviously not that busy.'

So we are none of us (obviously) too busy to constantly check how all the areas of our business are doing.

PEOPLE: HOW GOOD. HOW HAPPY. HOW MUCH POTENTIAL?

In an up-and-running business, people typically account for half the costs. So, we'd better check how they are doing and how they could do better. But this is about more than money. When we talk about the 'risk' of hiring someone, be aware that they, in return, are talking about the 'risk' they're taking in that we may not help get the best out of them. They need to be made to feel important (because they are) and they need our time.

We need to praise their good qualities and help them solve issues that irritate others (like unpunctuality, breaking promises, not listening, not looking enthusiastic and – worst of all – not paying attention). Money spent on training them will very seldom be wasted. So keep measuring their performances. People want and need to know how they're doing. We need to review people twice a year. And retain those records. These reviews are important and we need to spend time doing them. We also need to show good manners in the way we do them.

SALES: ACTUAL, PROSPECTIVE, PIPELINE

Sales are the lifeblood of any business. The ability to generate sales – they used to call it 'rainmaking' – is critical, but we need to refine, more clearly, what we mean by sales.

First of all, we have (or should have) a sales forecast. That will have been created by a mix of history, assessment of the saleability of our product range, our human resources (how many sales people do we have and what capacity do they have?) and what is the state of the market and the competition. By the way, nothing is more stupid than to blithely assume every year will be a growth year…unless we have changed things to improve our sales capacity. But assuming we hit the sales forecast, assuming our costs are on forecast, we should hit the profit target. But sales are not just a big number, they are a big number broken down into smaller parts.

Every month that forecast and the pipeline need to be reviewed and the unidentified income needs to be broken down into *how likely it is to land* – for instance 80 per cent likely; 60 per cent likely; 40 per cent likely; and 20 per cent likely (or not very likely at all). Don't buy 'it's a cert boss' until it's formally contracted. And then *when* it's likely to be invoiced. *When* is a critical word in business.

People who sell are generally, and by necessity, optimists, who are prone to forecast sales figures greater than they achieve and happening sooner than they actually do.

MARGIN: MAINTAINING MARGIN IS THE KEY TO A GREAT BUSINESS

It's so easy to cut prices and reduce margin, but that can be idiotic. If our product sells for £10 and we allow our very nice buyer to buy it for £9 – that's just a 10 per cent discount – but we have in that moment of generosity potentially halved our profit margin.

We need to monitor our margins the whole time and keep an eye on that margin percentage.

The single thing that will help our business maintain its profitability is by establishing our pricing so it sustains the margin we need and then, being hard to budge in reducing it. Sadly, the thing that has happened in a lot of businesses in the quest to maintain margin is the deterioration of product quality by reducing cost or, as some people call it, 'cost engineering'.

In service businesses, where there's no expensive machinery to write down, life may be simpler, but the broad principles of ensuring the margin isn't eroded are the same. We need to monitor our margins the whole time and keep an eye on that margin percentage.

BIG QUESTION: If your margin is eroding, is your product or service good enough to justify its price? Go back to first principles and check your offering in the context of the competitive market.

REPUTATION: TRUST, ESTIMATION AND AFFECTION

Our real reputation springs from how much we are trusted, in what we do and in what we say and promise. Warren Buffett said, 'It takes 20 years to build a reputation and five minutes to ruin it'.

Being trusted is a precious possession. Being trusted in an uncertain business climate, where previously rock solid reliable institutions have undergone various versions of reputational collapse, is an even greater possession:

- First of all, how are we doing with our trade customers or our clients? We must measure how we score on a regular basis. An irritated sales person's thinking, 'why are you asking this?' and saying, 'don't worry everything is fine', is really no good at all if you want to have a reasonable handle on the trend in your customer relationships.

- How do our consumers feel about us? Are they getting warmer or cooler in their feelings? It's amazing how many people guess this or, more honestly, say they don't know. If we're one of those, we'd better take care because we're flying our expensive aircraft without radar. However crude our estimates, we need, with reasonable confidence, to be able to assess how our standing is with the most important people in our commercial lives.

We need to make sure we communicate freely with all our stakeholders – that's suppliers, banks, investors, friends, peers – people who have a stake in us, real or emotional. Information is the last thing most people get, and often, when they do eventually hear from us, it's not good news. We need to remember that sales and profit are always the main focus in a business, but remembering all those human investor/stakeholders is essential too.

Our business, once we start employing people, becomes increasingly dependent on them, so we should fan their flames of enthusiasm by keeping them well informed on a regular basis as to how things are going. We should celebrate success loudly and cheerfully.

One of the very best things in a small start-up is the feeling that we are all family. So let's behave like one. Celebrating birthdays with a present for whoever's just got older can be more motivating than a bonus. The morale of our people, not just their performance, is a productivity accelerator. We need to work on it, be sensitive to it and decide how we can regulate it.

INTUITION: THAT INNER VOICE (LISTEN TO IT)
After Daniel Kahneman's 2012 book *Thinking, Fast and Slow*, everyone has taken a new view about emotion in business. Not everything is about numbers and not every measurement is quantitative. We, the start-up owner or co-owner, are allowed to have feelings. So how do *we* feel? Are *we* enjoying it? Are *we* in good form? Most of all, how does the business honestly feel to us ? Is it going the way *we* want?

As the leader, it's up to us to change it if we want to or if we feel it's necessary. Our intuition and our feelings are important. We must listen to our gut.

Thinking

In running our own business we need to be proactive. We need to think about what might be in the future, not just what is in the present. We need to be ready for anything. We need to be able to try things, to discard things, to change our mind and to find solutions to everyone's problems. We are the boss. Bosses need to behave as though they're invincible. And they need to see further into the future than anyone else. Here's what John Tuld (played by Jeremy Irons), the boss of the bank in the film *Margin Call* (2011), said in describing the investment banking business as a 'Pass the Parcel' game:

> I'm here for one reason and one reason alone. I'm here to guess what the music might do a week, a month, a year from now. That's it. Nothing more.

Pivoting when we need to change

We've said a lot about the need to be agile and nimble-minded. We've said we need to be big enough and nimble enough to change our mind when circumstances change. We are not just business leaders. We are thought leaders. Does that sound too pretentious for a shop that's selling vegan food or a tech business with three desks in a co-working office? We don't think so. Because thought leaders are creators, builders and winners.

EXAMPLE: Thought leaders think their way out of problems. Like Scientific Interactive thought about how to educate a mostly non-scientific board of a company to understand a particular chemical reaction by, through using VR, seeming to actually stand in the middle of it happening.

Houston we have a problem

All start-ups have crises. We're in the early infancy stage and there's a lot to think about. Are we good in a crisis? Do we panic? Do we, as Ben Horowitz (author of *The Hard Thing About Hard Things*) confessed to doing, feel sick a lot of the time? Do we have vivid 'what if' imaginations where the worst possible scenario is always filling our mind? Calm down, take deep breaths. No one is going to die unless it's us having a heart attack brought on by our failing to stay calm and quietly think:

- Let's be clear about what exactly has gone wrong and what the possible consequences are. We mustn't blame anyone. This is *our* problem and blame is a waste of time. Post-mortems come later.

- Having got a grip on the problem, we must share it; share it with mentors, wise friends and other people who've been through comparable crises and challenges. We've both helped people in such situations.

- Having – if we can – a restorative snooze can be beneficial (things usually seem better after a sleep).

- Telling the truth to the aggrieved party and saying sorry, fixing whatever's wrong at whatever it costs (we can count the cost later) are all tactics that work.

A problem is seldom a crisis; a crisis is seldom a catastrophe; a catastrophe is seldom a disaster.

But if it is a disaster, we must be grown up, pick up the pieces and move on. But really it's seldom quite as bad as it looks at first.

Pop-ups help us learn to earn

The real message here is that 'pop-up thinking' has now become the norm. We've all become used to creating strawmen, to testing our prototypes, to creating a trial and seeing what happens. Tests used to be laborious and expensive. Now they're easy and they're cheap. A lot of us live in beta now, beta tests of pre-release games software to a select group of people who test the game in their own homes, has become a norm and even part of the typical gaming marketing programme.

We encourage people to think in pop-up terms during innovation sessions. In animation virtually anything seems possible. In fact, we have barely explored the exciting possibilities that science and technology allow. It's a rotten time to be a cynic today, and we feel especially sorry for any cynical start-up. They'd better stop now – either their cynicism or the start-up.

Thinking styles

We are, of course, allowed to have different moods. No one, not even the most cockeyed of optimists, is a 100 per cent optimist all the time. We just need to decide what sort of thinking mode we are in at any moment of time.

Are we a realist? Do we generally think about things a bit sceptically, assuming the worst whilst hoping for better things? Do we need to know and grasp all the downsides? We know what we know but what we don't know yet, we need to understand and envisage what the Black Swans might be (a 'Black Swan' is an event that comes as a complete surprise, has a major effect, and is often inappropriately rationalized after the fact with the benefit of hindsight). A realist won't worry about them but will want to know if something really unexpected happens, how exposed they are and whether a cushion has been built into the plan.

Are we an ambitious optimist? Do we think about a glorious future? Do we want to know what the business will look like if everything goes right? Do we love the idea of blitz-scaling growth? The kind of expression that people like this relish is 'the size of the prize' and will ask questions like, 'What do we need to grow? How much do we need to invest? Who do we need to hire to win big?' Optimists tend to be alpha male and enjoy westerns and films like *Top Gun* (the classic Tom Cruise movie of 1986 about the Top Gun Naval Fighter Weapons School where the best of the best train to refine their elite flying skills).

Are we a creative? Do we get our kicks, not from money but thinking hard and filling blank sheets of paper with doodles, stray thoughts or anything that comes to mind? These people have dreams and are dream chasers. The chase matters more to them than anything else. Most inventors are dream chasers. Some like James Dyson actually get rich by dream chasing. What drives creatives is the 'next new thing' and creating something that's different, better and smarter than what already exists.

Are we a pragmatist? These are people who think about how to fix things, whose thrill is finding an ingenious solution. Lawyers are often pragmatists in seeing how to resolve an intransigent problem by finding examples of how previously such problems were solved. If we have a pragmatist on our team, we're lucky. These people think long and hard about how to simplify things, how to reduce cost and how to make things run more smoothly. They want to think things through properly. They do not chase dreams.

Keeping motivated to win, change and innovate

We need to look after our own motivation and sense of excitement. Let's face it, if we're starting a business we're probably going to be a pain in the neck, self-centred and wanting to talk about little else.

So, we need two things: distraction and inspiration.

We need to be able to stop working and give our busy brains a rest from time to time. We need to slow down and ponder, not constantly rush at life. We need to be distracted. But we also require inspiration outside our business.

We need to fill our head with ideas, thoughts and images. The essence of creativity has always been the knack of making surprising or original connections. We need to read books, watch films, watch the best of TED talks on YouTube, become a sponge. There's so much going on in cities, in shops, online, in hotels, in airports, in magazines or newspapers. We need to devour news, opinion and insights. There's a torrent of novelty out there to tickle our creative urges and keep our own ambitions and hopes in perspective.

We need role models as well as mentors. We should choose a few whom we can empathize with and enjoy. We should read their autobiographies, articles about them and watch them on videos.

People

'People are not your most important asset. The right people are', according to Jim Collins, author of *Good to Great.*

We shall keep on saying again and again that working with the right people is the key to success. If we hire people, the care and spirit with which we do this and the way we inspire and manage them will make a huge difference. If we don't hire people at the outset and *we're* the business, just us, all by ourselves, how we look after ourselves will be critical.

And as regards relationships, a successful business needs to get on well with *all* the people who work with it, invest in it, hire it to do work or in any way are in touch with it.

Looking after yourself

When we talked about this, we felt the need to shy away from the puritanical self-help advice we might read in a tabloid newspaper. What start-ups wanted, we thought, was something helpful to people, like us, who've started businesses and didn't look after ourselves very well at all. As we re-enacted scenes from *Mad Men*, drinking too many dry martinis or, joy of joys, found we were pitching for a booze account so we could sit at our desks swigging Drambuie at 11am and saying seriously, 'honestly, we're working', we were abusing our poor, overworked bodies rather irresponsibly. Here are four things that make a difference:

1 **Sleep**. Get seven to eight hours' sleep a night. Four hours' sleep followed by a workout at the gym as Harriet Green, now CEO of IBM Asia claims to do, seems to us insanity. Just don't go around looking knackered. Try to catch snoozes on planes and trains. Snoozes are the secret to success. Ask any busy, successful business person.

2 **Don't get hungry**. When our blood sugars get low, we go into an intellectual nosedive. If we're rushing around, we should try

Leon for a grease free, instantly served delicious snack. Now with 50 odd branches, it was set up by two Bain consultants in 2004 who got hacked off by the greasy, indigestible fast food then on offer. And remember, the occasional lunch is a wonderful way of creating good working relationships. People will tell us things when relaxed over lunch that they'd never tell us in an office.

3 **Exercise.** 'Whenever I feel the need to take exercise I sit down until it passes away.' That's what Billy Butlin, the holiday camp supremo, said. But busy people need to exercise in moderation. The great thing is we are our own boss, so we can take the decisions on how to spend our time. We are great believers in walking and talking. Walking helps us think. Walking helps us breathe. Walking stretches our minds and our bodies.

4 **Getting away.** It's madness not getting away for a no-work break. Our communication devices mean we're never completely cut off from phone or email if there is an urgent problem. If all we do is to get away briefly, we'll be better when we get back. Just taking a few days off wandering around Dorset or Suffolk or – better – a week on a Greek island staring at what Homer called 'the wine dark sea', drinking the wine dark wine and we'll be transformed.

Hiring and managing people

Some people, like Adam Spence, have said it wasn't until they started hiring people that they felt like a real business. There's something about walking in and your employees saying 'Morning Boss' in that ironic form of mock-cheeky greeting that makes us realize this is real, that we're in charge.

Getting HR processes right. We can no longer be casual about this. Verbal agreements are not good enough. In a litigious world we need to have proper contracts with everyone we hire. Hiring and firing is serious stuff. If we have to fire someone and we get the process wrong, we may find we are in a tribunal where we discover our carelessness results in an expensive mess. In the worst case scenario, being saddled with a large payment to the ex-employee could cost us the business. Good practice and good advice means this should be avoidable.

Hiring. People are interesting (nearly all of them), so interviews where we're enthusing about our business and seeing if their enthusiasm for life matches ours, are enjoyable. We must be clear in broad terms what we're looking for. In our experience it's attitude that matters most. We can coach skills. It's harder to coach attitude. So the attitude needs to be right. They should be bright, enterprising and can-do.

Whatever else, we must take our time. It's less important to fill a slot and much more important to hire the right person. We both, in our separate business lives, preferred to do things ourselves rather than hire someone expediently who wasn't really up to it, wouldn't be happy and would take too long to coach properly.

Telling them how they're doing and coaching them. In the early days they are not going to be as good as us; it would be unreasonable to expect that. So our task is to regularly tell them what they are great at and to work with them on the other stuff that lets them down. We need to show we care and are interested in them. We should not make them feel they are constantly under unreasonable pressure and being criticized and undervalued. At the beginning our team will be small. We must get the best out of them and accelerate their progress. If our attitude and their attitudes are both positive, it's amazing at how fast good things can happen.

We should formally evaluate them every six months so we both agree on how they are doing and what improvements are needed. If the improvement doesn't happen and the attitude worsens so they seem disinclined or unable to improve, these formal appraisals will be important evidence if they decide to get awkward when they're fired.

Let's remember this though. It's our aim never to part company on bad terms. Better to be more generous in our termination settlement and shake hands and remain friends. But if possible, let's try to coach people to be winners. Money spent on coaching people is seldom a waste of money. Some of it can be done internally and we, 'the boss', must be prepared to be Head Coach. Coaching, like marketing, is an investment but with a faster payback.

Creating 'team start-up'. Virtually everyone we know wants to be part of a winning team. Young people in businesses talk about 'my team' with, often, almost tribal intensity. It's our job to inspire our team to pour themselves into work each day and to love being there. No, this is not overly emotional at all. People want to be team players where their roles are clear and where they are valued and important. It's our team so let's be an inspirational leader of it and the energy source that drives the team to work harder with intensifying self-belief.

Looking after your stakeholders. We need to look after those stakeholders who'll pressurize us, care about us or worry about us. We mustn't be lazy; we need to be proactive and do things like remembering their birthdays. For many of them, including our bank, what we're doing may seem unusually adventurous. We recall that Monty Python sketch when Michael Palin improbably says he wants to be a lion tamer. That's what we're doing, it would seem to many, behaving like a lion tamer. Let's be natural, avoid jargon, be relaxed and kind and just tell them our news, good and if necessary, not so good. The things to avoid (especially with bankers, funders or any professional advisers) are nasty surprises.

Business is all about people. There's a phrase 'what goes round comes round' that is from the Karma law of cause and effect and about reaping what you sow. How you treat people tends to rebound on you, good or bad. Being congenitally good-natured is a good start to getting that Karma cycle moving the right way.

Customers

This is not the place to give a definitive lecture on marketing – that takes more time, and anyway there are whole books devoted to the subject (such as *Brilliant Marketing* by Richard Hall). This is a brief introduction to the key things we should focus on. We'll be very busy without trying (if we aren't already) to become a master (or mistress) marketeer as well as a star entrepreneur.

Our marketing plan

This is an essential part of any business plan (see earlier in this chapter). Too many good products or ideas fail because not enough of the people who would have liked them, got to hear about them. Great products that merely escape onto the market are seldom captured by their target market. Very few people understand marketing, especially finance people, some of whom seem to believe that it's some kind of commodity that you can measure by how much it costs, not what it says or how persuasive it is.

Marketing is part art, part science, part opinion, part fact. The power of a great idea that captures people's imagination is exponentially more effective than a reasonable idea. As one of the greatest advertising people of all time, Bill Bernbach, founder of the US advertising agency, DDB Ltd, said:

> Just because your ad looks good is no insurance that it will get looked at. How many people do you know who are impeccably groomed…but dull?

Bernbach's sayings are extensive and have gone into advertising folklore.

RULE ONE OF MARKETING: Never be dull. Never, ever be dull.

A proper marketing strategy

A strategy is a plan for success. We can take it that, as a start-up, we're going to be strapped for cash so, as Lord Rutherford, the father of nuclear physics put it, 'we have no money so we shall have to think'.

Our strategy will be simple (*it must be simple*):

WHO, precisely, are we targeting?

WHY should they listen to us?

WHAT do we want them to know, think and feel about our product or service?

HOW MUCH can we afford to spend?

Targeting our customers and creating momentum

Too many people say they want to reach 'everyone', which is as ridiculous as trying to reach the speed of sound in a Fiat 500. Target precisely. If we have a premium tea, we should be aiming at heavy premium tea drinkers who'll be able to discriminate when they discover a superior product. They'll be better off (after all, it's premium priced), but if some of them do all their shopping in Waitrose, who've refused to list us, forget about those. In his latest book *This is Marketing*, Seth Godin, prolific author and thinker, whom we've quoted several times because what he says is so relevant to small businesses, says:

> To start, first determine who your target audience is, develop buyer personas based on that audience, then market specifically to them. Solve their problems and answer their questions. By doing so, you'll build their trust, and eventually their hard-earned money.

So, let's try to get into the shoes and the heads of those most likely to try us and become regulars. Having got this far, determine to make them our brand champions. Set ourselves targets for achieving brand awareness amongst those who matter most to the business. Target levels of trial. Understand why levels of repeat purchase are as they are. Get immersed in the 'arithmetic of consumer behaviour'. For sure this won't be exact or scientific research – we are merely suggesting two things:

- Building a small but growing and articulate group of lovers of our brand is a priority.

- Creating a sense of growing momentum in sales or word of mouth is the key to success (just as the quantity of likes on social media is a key matrix).

'Momentum' is that hard-to-define sense of groundswell and of approval on the move. It's what – above all – small brands should be looking to achieve as the key to successful marketing.

Marketing tactics: the things we do to drive up sales

We have a small budget so we'd better 'think' and spend it wisely. If this means we have to do a lot of face-to-face, 'charm-them' sampling of our product, fine. Let's be creative and find ways of having 'conversations' with the sort of people we had in mind when we originally came up with our product idea.

We should never spread our money too thinly. We're better off creating a big noise in a small room than a whisper in a big room, because if we're inaudible we'll be wasting our money.

We'll get a lot of advice from very good marketeers, but many of them are just experienced at spending ample supplies of money, not working with small budgets. We should never take advice that we sense is spreading the butter too thinly on our marketing toast.

Marketing collateral or stuff like that

We need to make sure that we feel happy that our cards, logo, letterhead and website do our business justice. One of the things we've been advised to do in the past is to have a double-page spread advertisement designed that is our manifesto. 'Why I thought the world deserved a better mayonnaise' (or whatever it is you've invented), which is a great handout and can be included in our website. This is one of those illusory pieces of marketing, because only big confident companies would ever produce such a thing. It doesn't matter that it will never actually appear in any expensive medium. It's big, it looks important, it's beautiful and it's about us.

About digital presence and tactics (don't get too excited)

The conversations about digital will of course go on and on; there are a lot of voices talking digital; there are over 25,000 marketing agencies in the UK doing that talking. It's an important topic. There's no doubt that the internet has allowed the cost of entry to the market to be vastly reduced.

The trouble with digital is its existence has allowed the market to become very crowded, but, worse, the data to support its effectiveness is at best dodgy. We are sceptics, although LinkedIn seems serious and real, but from Facebook downwards we are unpersuaded. Be careful because there's a lot of snake oil in marketing and the digital world seems especially slippery.

Finding the right thing to say and the right way of saying it is much more important than where you say it.

We'd never invest money on a digital whim or if we weren't sure whether it made common sense. And, by the way, please don't talk about digital strategy. Digital is another medium not a panacea. Finding the right thing to say and the right way of saying it is much more important than where you say it.

Learning how to market cheaply and effectively

The key is to think small.

The big corporates can afford to splash money around, but it's not their money. In our start-up it's our money we're spending. Google Europe's HQ in Zurich is home to a mighty company, but it feels and it thinks small. They get carpet for their little sports room made from offcuts from a supplier donated free of charge, producing an attractive patchwork. Their table tennis table, table football and everything else are reclaimed and cost nothing. When we last looked, Google was valued at around US $800 billion, yet they think small and they think mean.

Remember Lord Rutherford? Think. Be clever. Be creative. Do something that makes people notice. Invest in a young local celebrity with the sort of money that would pay for a junior member of staff and make them an articulate champion like, for instance, a female golf player looking to go professional. Check out champion golfer Georgina Hall to see how much exposure she gets.

Thinking small doesn't mean thinking unambitiously, but it is probably rather unfamiliar (if we've previously worked for a big company). We are not apostles of austerity, but we are enemies of waste and ill-thought-through, speculative ideas.

Having a proper detailed sales plan

It's curious that the occupation of selling has, with some people, a slightly derogatory association, because without sales we get nowhere. To describe someone as a 'bit of a salesman' is not a compliment. As of now, right now, we are saying that's over, that selling is great, it's exciting and it's vital. We should tear up that beautifully crafted, literate and comprehensive business plan if we can't sell.

In a start-up the first and most critical thing is sales. No sales, no anything.

Planning, prospecting and good selling

The people best at selling plan their year, by month, week, day and hour. The essence of good sales people is their ability to plan, prioritize and be realistic as to how much can be achieved and how much time that will take. The sales plan stretches a year ahead because a lot of the biggest sales successes take that long to finalize.

The best sales people build a list of prospects and spend as much time researching them as they do selling. This means they know what they've done, how they're doing and what they seem to want. Prospects are not names on a list that we don't know. They are people who 'trust' us – that trust word again – when we meet because we've bothered to find out a lot about them. The longer that list, the harder we need to work at refreshing it and keeping in touch. Because, first of all, we value the power of relationships and regard the sale as a product of the relationship.

The best sales people do great sales presentations that are energetic, informed and clear. An OK presentation isn't good enough. It has to be great and it has to be persuasive. It must, in short, 'sell'. To get a real sense of salesmanship, read Malcolm Gladwell's (2009) description of Ron Popeil, the Ronco founder, at work on QVC. It's riveting. His one key lesson is to always ensure the 'product is the star'.

The best sales people always ask for feedback. They want to improve and know how to do that. They also know that people to whom they're selling are flattered by their asking them as an expert what tips they have. 'How could I do better?' is what everyone should be asking every day.

A sale isn't a sale until it's cash in the bank.

The best sales people will always ensure they have control of a pipeline of business so they control the contacts and presentations with various levels of likelihood of their becoming invoiced sales. We need to know who's on our list, how probable the sale is and when it'll happen. Will it be invoiceable in tranches or up front or what? A sale isn't a sale until it's cash in the bank.

Good selling means looking to the long term because it's based on two things. The building of a real relationship and the ability to have straight conversations. When the relationships are strong, the sales pitch can often be a chat between people who trust and like each other.

Measuring how we're doing with our customers

In the long run we want to have partners not customers, we want to be an adviser not a supplier, we want to be a friend not an adversary. Good conversations about how to improve our service can turn into a selling opportunity.

That's why we should regularly and formally do an update on how we can improve our service so we both do more business. This is the key. We are both on a mutual quest – to help the other win. Every year we should have a more detailed conversation about what we can do to make our customer more successful. The key question is 'how can we both do better by working *together*?'

There are two issues that need to be faced up to. Are there any things that impede our relationship from being a brilliant one? If so change them. Second, are there any opportunities we could make happen?

A long questionnaire is the wrong way to go about this. A business owner to business owner conversation is what's needed, probably over breakfast (the underestimated business meal), or a relaxing lunch where you need to be listening very carefully. The key is to be relaxed and extract the truth.

Being the greatest at customer service (your number one aim)

Being good at customer service is about being well mannered, attentive and recognizing our customer is always right. We are the provider and the customer nowadays expects zero defects in what we do. If a defect occurs, how we deal with it will determine our future relationship. Even if we inherit a situation where the relationship seems terrible we shouldn't panic. Here's what Bill Gates said (quoted in 'Smart Business Trends'):

> Your most unhappy customers are your greatest source of learning.

But only if we have an honest face-to-face conversation with them to find out *exactly* what's wrong, fix it and then tell them what we've done and thank them for their understanding.

We have to create a can-do, we-love-customers culture in our business. It's rather odd that so many people in business think it matters who's in the right when something goes wrong – the customer or them. *Anyway, the customer is always right* because they're paying the bill and by placing the order that they've trusted you to get right. In handling complaints we need to show we take them really seriously. A money-off-next-purchase voucher is worth less than a call from someone senior or a hand-written apology from the Chairman.

The only thing that matters is fixing what's wrong, not blaming anyone.

Say sorry if you're wrong.

Lawyers tell us not to say 'sorry'. Research in the United States about unhappiness in the legal profession is devastating, with many associates becoming disillusioned, cynical and dropping out. We shouldn't always listen to these miserable souls. Say sorry if you're wrong.

Running our business beyond start-up

Managing a sustainable business properly

This subject is of course a book in its own right, but here are a few tips. The assumption is that our start-up has started well so we must be doing something right. It's time to make sure we're positioned to become a grown-up, scaled-up company.

Grown-up management

There are four keys:

1 organization;
2 planning;
3 people;
  a. staff;
  b. customers;
4 new business.

The right organization saves time, frustration and tears

Too many companies have people wandering around not quite sure what everyone else is doing. Positions, accountability and line reporting are, over time, often fudged and no one has the courage to introduce clarity for fear of putting a few noses out of joint. It's time to put that right and be clear. Who does what? Who reports to whom? We need to make sure we have a machine that works properly. In the long run, a few tears are worth enduring if everyone (at last) knows what they are meant to be doing.

Without a proper planning process, you'll go mad

We cannot run a business into growth unless we manage all the key components. We believe this requires a cyclical not a linear approach. Every quarter we should focus on these in order. They go in the diary as seasonal planning cycles like spring, summer, autumn and winter, with specific review dates, like annual anniversaries. These could, for example, be as follows:

Review One – Sales and margin

Review Two – People, morale and alignment

Review Three – New business and innovation

Review Four – Customers – customer service

This doesn't mean we should only deal with each in that quarter, because that would be silly as each component requires ongoing attention, but in the specific quarter assigned to it the spotlight goes on initiatives, research and strategic as opposed to tactical thinking on the allocated topic. This happens every year. Every year without fail. What this does is force the key executives and non-executives to take proactive positions on the key issues rather than just reacting to the latest crisis.

People: THE KEY ASSET

Sam Walton, the founder of Walmart, said this, one of his many quotable quotes:

> Outstanding leaders go out of their way to boost the self-esteem of their personnel. If people believe in themselves, it's amazing what they can accomplish.

So we've got to do that. We also have to recognize the way we treat our people is going to be reflected in the way they treat their customers. In running a growing business we must ensure our HR processes are sound and that our management/ people attitudes are positive and inspiring, so we build a tribe of people who like coming into work and go home in a good mood.

This may sound very idealistic, but isn't it time to start being nicer to each other?

Peter Mead was Founder and key director of Abbott Mead Vickers, the UK's most successful advertising agency for many decades. It's an extraordinary success story. He wrote a book about it. It's called *When in Doubt Be Nice*. Go figure.

You can't scale up without winning a lot of new business

Whether we're an advertising or a PR agency, a fintech, a pie maker, a designer, a consultant or a retailer, a large proportion of our lives is going to be spent trying to win more business or persuading people to do things that are good for us. Both of us have spent a lot of our respective business lives in competitive pitches trying to win budgets from new clients.

What we both needed to do was pitch more effectively – reducing wasted time, enhancing our chances of winning and building a Presentation Machine.

A guide to presenting for new business

LEARNING TO SAY 'NO'

We must focus on trying to win the business that we have the most chance of winning. We shouldn't chase long-shots at the expense of low-hanging fruit, however glamorous those long-shots might seem. And if the brief seems beyond our reach and capabilities right now, we should say 'no' to the opportunity and work out how to plan, strategically, to build our capabilities so that we're ready next time around.

CHECK OUT THAT IT'S A WINNING PRESENTATION

We should always sense-check our presentation with peers or mentors. We need to stand apart from the process and to weigh the outcome against what they believe the client needs, wants and thinks.

The only presentation worth bothering with is one that has a great chance of winning. Doing one that we believe is right in absolute terms but unbuyable by a client or customer is an utter waste of time.

Ask yourself this question – is this a winning pitch from the potential customer's viewpoint?

KEEPING OUR PITCH CONCISE

The most effective way to reduce time-wasting in the pitch process is also the simplest – we should create our pitch to fit the time we have (not the time we wish we had). At a very early stage, we should ask how long we will have to pitch. We should always be ready to do the brilliant 'five-minute' pitch and ditch the longer version in case the customer's schedule changes.

HAVING A PITCH TEAM

This is not all about us as leader. Our job is to lead, to manage but not to be 100 per cent hands on. Our job (if possible) is to have one-to-one meetings with the potential customer's top person before the presentation and again after it. Our team will be the people who create the relationship on a day-to-day basis.

We recall times when (immodestly) we thought we personally played a blinder but, after winning the business, found it was a day-to-day junior who'd won over the junior client who had day-to-day accountability for the business, who'd really secured victory.

WE MUST HAVE A PROCESS
Every sales presentation should include six elements:

1 What the customer/client has told us about themselves.

2 What we've done to find out more.

3 Focusing on the key problems.

4 Focusing on the key opportunities.

5 How we'd help realize those opportunities...this is the magic section.

6 Why we'd be such a great partner.

There's no need to be boringly regimented, but the thrust of virtually every presentation contains proof that we're smart, that we understand the business and that we want to help them succeed.

PLAN, THINK, EMPATHIZE AND VISUALIZE
We need to do the work, the research, the field trips, the interviews with client staff, the examination of their competitive landscape. We need in short to understand their business because – and this is fundamental – *we should want to position ourselves as business partners and advisers not just as a supplier.*

We must understand how they feel and what they think they need, be a sympathetic, listening audience and remember this quote, thought to be from Maya Angelou:

> I've learned that people will forget what you said, people will forget what you did, but people will never forget how you made them feel.

IS OUR CHEMISTRY RIGHT?

If it isn't, it'll show. People who might be working with, relying on or being supplied by us want to see happy, relaxed and motivated teams. It's the 'chemistry' that influences 80 per cent of pitch decisions according to The Future Factory's survey on new business presentations. If we are creating a world of pain, for ourselves and our team, it's inevitable that this will translate into the pitch presentation, and we are, then, really wasting our time.

WE MUST UNDERSTAND HOW TO WIN

In a pitch presentation it is not just the top woman or man alone who counts, it's all the people there whom we'll be working with daily. These people will be going back to HQ, an ordinary office or the factory afterwards and their reaction to what they tell them will make the relationship be a good or less good one.

Four things are key:

1 **Give them portable ideas**. Our idea needs to be instantly communicable outside the presentation with clients or customers. Anyone needs to be able to summarize our idea in two or three sentences at the most, so we must give the client a narrative that works in a snatched conversation in the corridor.

2 **Trust** is probably the most underrated but important quality in winning a pitch. It's trust that seals the deal. In his book *The Trusted Advisor*, David H Maister presents a formula for any consultant in the business of serving clients or customers and looking to improve the level of trust:

   Trust is a combination of: credibility, reliability and intimacy divided by the perceived level of your own self-interest that you communicate to the client.

3 **Do we have credibility?** Our track record, our experience and our real relevance to a customer's business are all important. But we must make sure these qualities are highly attuned to

the client's own specific situation. We must make sure they feel we fit with them culturally and that we are not perceived as too grand, too flash, too busy or just too greedy.

4 **Are we reliable?** We can make sure we are communicating reliability through all stages of the pitch process, from promptly returning phone calls to turning up to meetings at allotted times, to appearing to be prepared to work harder than other contestants.

Always ask 'what's next?'

The reason we wanted to start a new business was to achieve freedom and control of our lives. It seems too often that businesses falter as they mature because the founders get bored. What started as a thrill can become routine and dull. But an essential characteristic of a successful business is how it creates and manages change. People who work there need new challenges, new jobs and promotions. Everyone needs to see the momentum created by the launch of new products and the winning of new customers and clients.

An essential characteristic of a successful business is how it creates and manages change.

Every business needs to question constantly how they can improve, become more innovative and do something that has business peers frustrated and impressed. The worst response to the question 'how are things going?' is the languid 'same as, same as'. Change matters because it shakes everyone up from time to time.

At some moment, we'll face options that may include an exit and a cashing-in, a restructuring to reward and motivate our most talented people, a plan to accelerate growth and achieve a major scale-up or, possibly, a merger or a take-over. Change for change's sake is not the idea, but it's a fact that change is inevitable, so it's better to be there managing it, before it happens to us, rather than be forced to react when we least expect to have to do so.

We believe there is no better way than the creation of account-able profit centres, because it's by giving people operational accountability and the resources to innovate, grow and become exceptional that great things can happen.

But this world, thrilling as it, is changing very fast and we can only legitimately philosophize against this background and within this context. We must be more attuned to what is happening in the wider world, to competitive activity, to new trends, fashions and tastes, to new thinking. Sergeant Stan Jablonski in the TV classic *Hill Street Blues* used to end his briefings to his team:

Let's do it to them before they do it to us.

Well, let's shall we? Otherwise we'll be in danger of being history.

The story of an award-winning success

An interview with Rachel Bell by Richard Hall

Rachel is dyslexic, which has shaped the way she works. She listens with the concentration that others use when reading. She has a visual imagination rather than a literary one. She is a maven, enthusing about the synergy of putting the right people in contact with each other and is always up for new conversations. Her appetite for life, for people, for laughing and for partying are legendary. She thinks Shine was a winning business in part because it was more fun than other PR agencies (and so it was in the days of advertising in which I lived, when fun mattered more than it seems to today).

First of all some background.

She learnt how business worked early on from her father who'd founded an engineers' merchant and talked about his business constantly at home. Entrepreneurs are often nurtured young. She was never going to be an academic and started her working life in hotels, at the Tara and then the Hyatt. She discovered that the more you did and the more initiative you showed, the faster you got promoted. She said it was obvious that, 'execution is the real key. However good an idea, it means nothing if it doesn't get done well'.

She made a move into PR to the large firm Fleishman Hillard, starting at the bottom. There she spent three years graduating from account executive to account director, but she was never, she felt, quite trusted in front of clients. When presenting with her boss, she says, she gushed garbage but on her own she was articulate and authoritative. It was on her own that she won and then ran the Dunlop Slazenger account. She loved it and it went well. When it wasn't profitable enough for the agency, her boss, out of the blue and without telling her what he planned to do, resigned the business. She was outraged and she immediately resigned too.

'It was an absolute matter of principle. I didn't have to think twice', she says. She tossed up between being a waitress – 'I liked the hospitality business and I was fed up' – or starting her own agency. Her dad was ill, life was crazy, she was confused and so decided to try her own thing. She says she even took a call asking her to pitch for business just as her dad's funeral was about to start.

So what were the keys to her success at creating her businesses? I tell her I need a list of say 10 essentials – 'there's more than 10', she says, in the tone of someone used to getting her own way. 'No just 10', I say.

If these tips are already in the book, well a bit of repetition never did any harm, not if it's good stuff. Rachel stops laughing – '10', she says, puts down her glass of wine and thinks. She explains her agency was called Shine because of Nelson Mandela's inauguration speech in 1994:

> And as we let our own light shine we consciously give other people permission to do the same.

1 **Don't do what you can't.** She says she's never ever sent out an invoice. Her first hiring was a bookkeeper because, 'I didn't understand that stuff'. But she understood the important numbers and always tracked those.

2 **I was selling time not just ideas.** You have only so much time to work with and you can't sell more than 75 per cent of it or there's nothing in reserve and your business runs out of puff.

3 **Ours is a ratio game.** It's very simple. Fifty per cent of the income pays for salaries; 30 per cent pays for offices, admin and all that support overhead; 20 per cent is your profit. Live with that as your model and you won't go wrong. (Sir Martin Sorrell agrees with this model. It ruled WPP.)

4 **People are the real key.** Fifty per cent of the money goes on them, but they produce 100 per cent of the difference, so listen to them, hear what they are saying, all of them, because everyone matters.

5 **Be attractive.** Early on she pitched the Shine story to all the head hunters making sure that they all knew Shine was going to be a great place to work. She was determined people would never leave with bad feeling and that everyone (suppliers, media, clients, staff) felt 'the magic'.

6 **Creating a folklore is how to make a brand.** You need to find new stories the whole time. Unless your business can have the reputation where people say – 'only at Shine or only at FCO', you aren't creating the brand illusion of being 'the special ones'.

7 **It's all about the team…TEAM. TEAM. TEAM.** When individuals become more important than the team, you have a big problem. The biggest enemy to a start-up is **EGO**.

8 **Create relationships. Transactions come much later.** It's who you know and how well you get on with them that, one day in the future, may allow you to make a call that saves you from a disaster or opens the door to a triumph.

9 **Be a 'resource investigator'.** Be curious about life. Use 'why?' a lot. Seek out interesting people and interesting things. Leave room in your life to discover amazement.

10 **Feel good. Do good. Spread good.** Idealistic? Maybe it is, but your reputation is everything, your disciples are your best sales people and doing good things for others refreshes the soul and brightens your image.

OVERARCHING PHILOSOPHY

Grow talent, make it shine and when it's ready, encourage people to take ownership of their own profit centres. Shine has become a kindergarten for some of London's best PR talent and best PR agencies.

THE SUCCESSES

1999 – Shine in its first year was *PRWeek*'s Best New Agency.

2003 – Shine was *Marketing Magazine*'s Agency of the Year.

2009 – Mischief (a Shine spin-off) was *PRWeek*'s Best Agency.

2011 – Mischief was *PRWeek*'s Best Mid-sized Agency.

2012 – Shine was the *Sunday Times* Best Small Company to Work For in the UK.

2012 – John Doe (a Shine spin-off) was *PRWeek*'s Agency of the Year and Best Boutique Agency.

2014 – Aduro Communications (a Shine spin-off) was Best New Agency finalist.

2016 – John Doe New York was *PRWeek US*'s Best New Agency.

CHAPTER SIX

Conclusions and summary

Why this book matters

We, between us, have around three-quarters of a century of learning. In our respective lifetimes we have never seen so perfect a storm of change, so perfect a landscape in which to plant a new business. In our experience uncertainty has a much more destabilizing effect on big, bureaucratic businesses than on small, nimble ones.

When you start a new business you change the world, just a little, but you change it. It's not easy to succeed, which makes it all the more thrilling when you do win a new customer or introduce an attention-getting new product.

Here are our key lessons, learnings and insights that have appeared in *Start-ups, Pivots and Pop-ups*. Regard them as a tasting menu. What's excited us is what we have learnt from our many interviews and discussions. We salute the skills, resilience and creativity of those who've helped us. With stars like these the next generation will do fine in the future.

Summary of the book: some key take-outs and thoughts

THERE IS A START-UP REVOLUTION

The word revolution is often used lightly. But we believe there are a series of factors currently that smell of revolution. The demographics and the mindsets developing in the workplace; the increasing bureaucratic constipation in big corporations; the signs of rebelliousness plus the current wave of creativity – all these say disruption and creative destruction are about to attack the sloppy, slack and reactionary.

WOMEN AND MILLENNIALS ARE CHANGING THE WORLD

The glass ceiling and the stories of female repression have been cheerfully contradicted by the women we've talked to who, having gained experience and skills, are starting up robust and well-thought through businesses. Everywhere we see change, in Asia, in Poland. Women are rewriting the rules.

The millennials, rather than being snowflakes, are providing an avalanche of evidence that the future belongs to them and on their terms. Many found the idea of working for a big business where they had menial roles unthinkable. Again, throughout the world, the idea of starting our own business seems normal, even in India where the smartest graduates go off to do their own thing now rather than joining Tata or Goldman Sachs.

WINNING IS ALL ABOUT 'ATTITUDE'

We believe you can teach new skills, but it's harder to create new attitudes. The entrepreneurial spirit requires courage, resilience and a collaborative spirit. In today's world, loners are getting lost. People who like people and get on with their customers and staff are more likely to succeed. People who have boundless energy and a can-do attitude are more likely to succeed. People who have a hunger to succeed, a vision of what success would look like and a lot of self-belief are more likely to succeed.

Add to that a sense of curiosity and a restless urge to learn and you have the perfect most-likely-to succeed entrepreneur.

START-UPS: THE SECRETS

Actually, they aren't secrets. They are just three important things to get right that many start-ups fail to pay attention to:

1 **Partnerships and people.** Business is always about people and the biggest reason businesses fail is because of relationship breakdowns – between partners, because of dysfunctional teams in the company, or because the bond of trust between a top team and its stakeholders has been severed for some reason. Spend time loving, helping and thinking about all your people.

2 **Customer focus.** Without understanding and paying attention to your customers' needs and changing needs, your start-up can neither start nor scale. Seth Godin preaches the need to focus on fewer customers. Build, he says, from a loyal core on whom you lavish attention rather than trying to mass market, which is expensive, exhausting and exceedingly old fashioned. We know that we need brand champions not just users. The current argument is to find products for your customers not customers for your products.

3 **Doing it properly**. There's no excuse for being sloppy. Starting a business is not a hobby. Everything you do from your business cards, to the way people answer the phone, to the way you handle complaints has to be exceptional, not just OK. The best businesses have a culture and a tribal intensity that began when they started up. Execution is the key. Every business needs great execution of its ideas. Imagine going to a restaurant where the raw ingredients were great, the menu fabulous but the cooking was only so-so. Make sure so-so is a concept alien to your business. There is no place for mediocrity in the 2020s.

POP-UPS: THE ART OF EXPERIMENTING

Innovation and experimentation. The essence of all start-ups is that they are innovative and designed to disrupt a market sector. Pop-ups are ideal, relatively low-cost ways of trying out new ideas. They also allow start-up owners to get closer to their ultimate consumers and learn from them. Since the late 2000s, we have seen the demise of fixed-in-their way retailers with large fixed costs being more focused on rental costs than on innovating and transforming their offering. The pop-up is the way to learn about what's new and different that inspires consumers.

PIVOTS: RESPONDING TO CHANGE

Strategic tweaking. A pivot is a change induced by a piece of learning or a change of circumstance. There are some fine examples in *Start-ups, Pivots and Pop-ups* of people who've realized they have got elements in their offering wrong and have changed it. We call this 'tacking' (as in sailing) in response to the wind of customer opinion. Refer to John Maynard Keynes who said, 'When circumstances change I change my mind. What do you do?' We pivot.

Crazy dreams. The most obvious pivot of all is to give up a well-paid job and start your own business. We have some fine examples of this from the United States and the UK. From State Prosecutor to advertising man or from entrepreneur to doctor. We are believers in following your dream. We think that careers, as we used to know them, are over. We believe that more people will be courageous enough to explore their skills and passions and make their crazy dreams a reality.

HOW TO MAKE A START-UP SUCCEED

Planning. Business plans are, in themselves, overrated, but the process by which they are produced is critical. In a start-up, thinking about how to create the future and what the obstacles to success might be, are essential elements in the journey to creating a solid, growing business. Most important of all is embedding planning into your business so, on a cyclical basis, the key elements of your business operation are minutely reviewed and improved. Finally, sales. Sales prospects need to be planned and a pipeline of potential business with a percentage probability of landing it needs to be in place and constantly reviewed. Optimism and fantasy when it comes to sales planning are often at the root of a business failing.

Execution. We talked about whether this section of the book wasn't a little prosaic or even dull. But given the demise of so many businesses is related to failures of execution not of concept, we decided 'crazy dreams' needed to be planted in a bed of fertile and consistent process. As the Oliver and Young song made famous by Ella Fitzgerald, and then later by Bananarama, goes:

> It ain't what you do it's the way that you do it, that's what
> gets results.

Momentum. Momentum is that magic energy a business has when people are talking about it, when sales start to accelerate, when journalists call, when likes on social media grow and when you are suddenly a bit overwhelmed by how busy things are. Momentum is fundamental to business success; you can sense it as you walk into a building; you can feel it in the air. Creating momentum is the most important marketing tool any start-up should have.

Money. We identified early on that it's mostly the men who control the money, and we loved that arch comment from Ruth Rochelle about when seasoned funders get involved, as businesses start to scale up. 'That', she said, 'is when idealism takes a kicking.' Increasingly people embarking on a start-up are funding it themselves. But as this 'start-up revolution' intensifies, the issue of funding will, we suspect, become less problematic as innovation and enterprise seem more attractive.

THE IMPORTANCE OF TIMING, LUCK AND PERSISTENCE

Timing is important. Do not rush to market. Get as many things right as possible. It's more important to be ready than to be first – although the imperative to get to market is more urgent in the tech space where first mover advantage is taken very seriously especially by funders. Bad timing is more often than not an excuse for 'not quite ready'. Be ready.

Luck. It's not helpful to talk about luck because it acknowledges that much of what happens is beyond our control. However, by creating momentum and by being proactive and just plain busy, we can at least be architects rather than victims of events.

Persistence and resilience are the hallmarks of successful entrepreneurs. Ambition and determination to succeed are critical. You are fighting for your life when you start a new business. So fight, don't give up. Just be prepared to put up with a few disappointments and keep going.

EVERYONE NEEDS A MENTOR

Do not be alone. Unless you have people around you to keep up your spirits, you could get very depressed. You need good advice, legal, financial, IT, marketing, but most of all you need a mentor. Someone who's experienced, empathetic and wise. The occasional uplifting conversation can transform your morale and your business.

FINAL ADVICE: ALWAYS BE AT LEAST JUST A BIT BETTER

Start-ups, Pivots and Pop-ups has plenty to say about business models, saying that the wrong model equals big trouble. But the one critical distinction a start-up business needs is to be better. How much better? Enough better than the competition to be noticed:

- better product;
- better service;
- better price;
- better packaging;
- better advertising;

- better people;
- better leadership;
- better initiatives;
- better momentum.

Review everything you do and don't ask 'is it good enough?'; ask 'is it better?'.

Finally, do you want to make a difference?
Do you want to feel wonderful?

Just read the words with which we started *Start-ups, Pivots and Pop-ups* and start to make your crazy dream real:

> Most people find their biggest disappointment in life is their caution – the things they didn't do, rather than those they did. We encourage you all to be bold, to dream, to explore your talent and to find your true potential as an independent spirit.

Bibliography

Prologue

Chouinard, Y (2016) *Let My People Go Surfing: The education of a reluctant businessman – including ten more years of business unusual*, Penguin, Harmondsworth

Cocconi, G and Morrison, P (1959) Searching for interstellar communications, *Nature*, **184** (4690), pp 844–6

Dowd, K [accessed 31 May 2019] Brighton, *Fleurets* [Online] www.fleurets.com/market-intelligence/2019/may/brighton (archived at https://perma.cc/FGX2-VY6X)

HSBC Business [accessed 31 May 2019] The Future of Business 2011 [Online] www.business.hsbc.co.uk/1/PA_esf-ca-app-content/content/pdfs/en/future_of_business_2011.pdf (archived at https://perma.cc/T75M-VQTL)

Sager, M [accessed 31 May 2019] Andy Grove: What I've Learned, *Esquire* [Online] www.esquire.com/entertainment/interviews/a1449/learned-andy-grove-0500/ (archived at https://perma.cc/95NE-ZFP7)

Chapter 1

Akalp, N [accessed 31 May 2019] How Entrepreneurial Baby Boomers Are Rethinking Retirement [Online] www.forbes.com/sites/allbusiness/2015/06/02/how-entrepreneurial-baby-boomers-are-rethinking-retirement/#5ed7ca4b10b0 (archived at https://perma.cc/J4C4-YZYS)

Carreyou, J (2018) *Bad Blood: Secrets and lies in a Silicon Valley startup*, Penguin Random House, New York

Chapman, B [accessed 31 May 2019] Fat Cat Friday: Just Six FTSE 100 CEOs Are Women and They Earn Half the Salaries of Male Counterparts [Online] www.independent.co.uk/news/business/news/fat-cat-friday-women-ftse-100-ceos-earn-half-salaries-men-a8710171.html (archived at https://perma.cc/2TH8-SB5G)

Cosic, M [accessed 31 May 2019] 'We Are All Entrepreneurs':
    Muhammad Yunus on Changing the World, One Microloan
    at a Time [Online] www.theguardian.com/sustainable-business/2017/
    mar/29/we-are-all-entrepreneurs-muhammad-yunus-on-changing-the-
    world-one-microloan-at-a-time (archived at https://perma.cc/
    PW65-ZQ47)

Heffernan, M (2008) *Women on Top: How women entrepreneurs
    are rewriting the rules of business success*, Penguin Books,
    New York

Milburn, M [accessed 17 January 2017] Politics and Jobs 'Swell Youth
    Anxiety' – Prince's Trust [Online] www.bbc.co.uk/news/
    education-38518543 (archived at https://perma.cc/ZMK3-RQYK)

Oxford Dictionary [accessed 31 May 2019] Definition of Entrepreneur
    [Online] https://en.oxforddictionaries.com/definition/entrepreneur
    (archived at https://perma.cc/6RUY-H6AU)

Parry, D [accessed 31 May 2019] Richer Sounds Founder Hands Control
    to Staff [Online] www.thetimes.co.uk/article/richer-sounds-chief-
    hands-workers-3-5m-windfall-n0nb0ml9r (archived at
    https://perma.cc/CG2A-B7LC)

Peters, T (2003) *Re-imagine! Business excellence in a disruptive age*, DK
    Publishing, London

Richer, J (2019) *The Ethical Capitalist: How to make business work
    better for society*, Random House Business, New York

Sanghera, S [accessed 31 May 2019] Dream of Being an Entrepreneur?
    Trust Me, They Dream of Being You [Online] www.thetimes.co.uk/
    article/dream-of-being-an-entrepreneur-trust-me-they-dream-of-being-
    you-cvxdtrx32 (archived at https://perma.cc/85G2-8YZF)

Sinek, S [accessed 28 February 2017] Millennials [Online] www.youtube.
    com/watch?v=hER0Qp6QJNU (archived at https://perma.cc/4YCN-
    TRWD)

Treanor, J [accessed 31 May 2019] Women Will Wait 217 Years for Pay
    Gap to Close, WEF Says [Online] www.theguardian.com/society/2017/
    nov/01/gender-pay-gap-217-years-to-close-world-economic-forum
    (archived at https://perma.cc/U4MS-4SUT)

Chapter 2

Block, F [accessed 31 May 2019] China Leads List of Self-Made Female Billionaires [Online] www.barrons.com/articles/china-leads-list-of-self-made-female-billionaires-1520538727 (archived at https://perma.cc/7R88-94JH)

Brinded, L [accessed 29 June 2019] The Nine Richest Self-Made Billionaires in the World, *Business Insider* [Online] www.businessinsider.com/hurun-global-self-made-women-billionaires-list-2017-3?r=US&IR=T (archived at https://perma.cc/LG75-NFW4)

Gluckman, D (2017) *That S*it Will Never Sell! A book about ideas by the person who had them*, Prideaux Press, New York

Haidt, J (2013) *The Righteous Mind: Why good people are divided by politics and religion*, Penguin, Harmondsworth

Harari, Y N (2011) *Sapiens: A brief history of humankind*, Vintage Publishing, New York

Heffernan, M (2008) *Women on Top: How women entrepreneurs are rewriting the rules of business success*, Penguin Books, New York

HSBC Business [accessed 31 May 2019] The Future of Business 2011 [Online] www.business.hsbc.co.uk/1/PA_esf-ca-app-content/content/pdfs/en/future_of_business_2011.pdf (archived at https://perma.cc/T75M-VQTL)

Kegan, R [accessed 31 May 2019] Uncovering Your Immunity to Change [Online] www.executiveinspiration.com/wp-content/uploads/2017/01/Immmunity-to-Change-Guide.pdf (archived at https://perma.cc/HL7A-J2LE)

Osnos, E (2015) *Age of Ambition: Chasing fortune, truth and faith in the new China*, Vintage Books, London

Pease, A and Pease, B (2002) *Why Men Don't Listen and Women Can't Read Maps*, Orion Books, London

Pink, D (2008) *A Whole New Mind: Why right-brainers will rule the future*, Marshall Cavendish, London

Sutherland, R (2019) *Alchemy: The surprising power of ideas that don't make sense*, WH Allen, London

Turtlewise [accessed 31 May 2019] Website [Online] https://turtlewise.net/ (archived at https://perma.cc/W3WC-75Y4)

Chapter 3

BBC News Website [accessed 31 May 2019] Q&A: The Enron Case [Online] news.bbc.co.uk/1/hi/business/3398913.stm (archived at https://perma.cc/LX6V-K2LG)

Collins, J C and Porras, J I (1994) *Built to Last: Successful habits of visionary companies*, William Collins, Glasgow

Gladwell, M (2009) *What the Dog Saw and Other Adventures*, Little, Brown and Company, Boston, MA

Godin, S (2018) *This is Marketing: You can't be seen until you learn to see*, Penguin, Harmondsworth

Goldwyn, S [accessed 8 July 2019] Never Make Forecasts, Especially About the Future [Online] www.forbes.com/quotes/author/samuel-goldwyn/ (archived at https://perma.cc/9RB2-MBBT)

Harari, Y N (2018) *21 Lessons for the 21st Century*, Jonathan Cape, London

Hoffman, R [accessed 3 November 2018] Interview with Adam Bryant, CNBC [Online] www.cnbc.com/video/2018/11/03/in-depth-interview-with-linkedin-co-founder-reid-hoffman.html (archived at https://perma.cc/UTF9-GGS9)

Holodny, E [accessed 31 May 2019] Warren Buffet Explains Why a Good Business is One 'Your Idiot Nephew' Could Run [Online] www.businessinsider.com/warren-buffett-good-business-could-be-run-by-idiot-2016-3?r=US&IR=T (archived at https://perma.cc/UQ4K-KMMB)

Kahneman, D (2012) *Thinking, Fast and Slow*, Penguin, Harmondsworth

Kim, L [accessed 31 May 2019] Why Startup Pivots Almost Never Work [Online] https://medium.com/the-mission/why-startup-pivots-almost-never-work-50bc66733b8c (archived at https://perma.cc/F2M3-YNAZ)

Lewis, M (2010) *The Big Short: Inside the Doomsday Machine*, W. W. Norton, New York

Love British Food Blog [accessed 31 May 2019] Producer of the Month: Jason Barber, Black Cow [Online] www.lovebritishfood.co.uk/blog/producer-of-the-month-jason-barber-black-cow-vodka (archived at https://perma.cc/MV95-ZZL7)

Oxford Dictionary [accessed 31 May 2019] Definition of Pivotal [Online] https://en.oxforddictionaries.com/definition/pivotal (archived at https://perma.cc/4RR3-Q4S7)

Ries, E (2011) *The Lean Startup*, Crown Publishing Group, New York

Samit, J (2015) *DISRUPT YOU! Master personal transformation, seize opportunity, and thrive in the era of endless innovation*, Flatiron Books, New York

Satara, A [accessed 31 May 2019] In Two Sentences Elon Musk Explains Why the Key to Success is Failure [Online] www.inc.com/alyssa-satara/ in-2-sentences-elon-musk-explains-why-key-to-success-is-failure.html (archived at https://perma.cc/HFZ4-VV3H)

Siddle, R [accessed 31 May 2019] *The Buyer* Was Able to Sit Down with Diane Hunter, Chief Executive of Conviviality PLC, and Michael Sanders, Chief Executive of Bibendum PLB, at Yesterday's London Wine Fair to Assess Exactly How the Two Are Going to Bring Their Two Businesses Together [Online] www.the-buyer.net/insight/the-buyer-was-able-to-sit-down-with-diane-hunter-chief-executive-of-conviviality-plc-and-michael-saunders-chief-executive-of-bibendum-plb-at-yesterdays-london-wine-fair-to-assess-exactly/ (archived at https://perma.cc/4RNR-B4YL)

Taylor, A [accessed 8 July 2019] Global Startup Ecosystem Report 2018 [Online] www.bbntimes.com/en/technology/global-startup-ecosystem-report-2018 (archived at https://perma.cc/2TTZ-MQ69)

Taylor, A [accessed 8 July 2019] The Startup Speaks: Al Taylor of Tootle [Online] www.thegoodwebguide.co.uk/article/al-taylor-tootle/18327 (archived at https://perma.cc/9QWM-MSA8)

The Producers (1967) dir. Mel Brooks

Welch, J (2003) *Jack: Straight from the gut*, Hachette, London

Chapter 4

Amazon [accessed 31 May 2019] Amazon Go – No Lines. No Checkout. (No, Seriously) [Online] www.amazon.jobs/en/business_categories/ amazongo?base_query=&loc_query=&job_count=10&result_limit= 10&sort=relevant&business_category%5B%5D=amazongo&cache (archived at https://perma.cc/X3L6-6PQG)

Baird, N [accessed 31 May 2019] Retail's Uberization is Already Here: It's Called Pop-Up Stores [Online] www.forbes.com/sites/nikkibaird/ 2018/03/26/retails-uberization-is-already-here-its-called-pop-up-stores/#745eb858c1aa (archived at https://perma.cc/29GF-82F2)

Blank, S [accessed 31 May 2019] Why Corporate Skunk Works Need to Die [Online] https://alopexoninnovation.com/2014/11/15/why-corporate-skunk-works-need-to-die/ (archived at https://perma.cc/2F66-6S96)

Bourdain, A (2004) *"Les Halles" Cookbook: Strategies, recipes, and techniques of classic bistro cooking*, Bloomsbury, London

Chesky, B [accessed 31 May 2019] Don't F*ck up the Culture [Online] https://medium.com/@bchesky/dont-fuck-up-the-culture-597cde9ee9d4 (archived at https://perma.cc/KUD2-XGSK)

Coren, G [accessed 31 May 2019] Giles Coren Reviews Duck Goose et al [Online] www.thetimes.co.uk/article/giles-coren-reviews-duck-duck-goose-et-al-2xkn6dlvn (archived at https://perma.cc/C3SU-EYMB)

Dufresne, S [accessed 31 May 2019] The IBM PC That Broke IBM [Online] https://hackaday.com/2017/12/11/the-ibm-pc-that-broke-ibm/ (archived at https://perma.cc/V6HF-2MBY)

Gilbert, D (2007) *Stumbling on Happiness*, Harper Perennial, New York

Gordon, L H [accessed 30 June 2019] Intimacy: The Art of Relationships [Online] www.psychologytoday.com/us/articles/196912/intimacy-the-art-relationships (archived at https://perma.cc/N4XB-2KMH)

Hoque, F [accessed 31 May 2019] Why Most Venture-Backed Companies Fail [Online] www.fastcompany.com/3003827/why-most-venture-backed-companies-fail (archived at https://perma.cc/UL6F-UVQM)

Horowitz, B (2014) *The Hard Thing About Hard Things: Building a business when there are no easy answers*, HarperBusiness, New York

IBM [accessed 31 May 2019] The Birth of the IBM PC [Online] www.ibm.com/ibm/history/exhibits/pc25/pc25_birth.html (archived at https://perma.cc/N3MJ-PKPW)

Sculley, J [accessed 31 May 2019] *Bloomberg Game Changers: Steve Jobs* [Online] https://signalvnoise.com/posts/2813-do-you-want-to-sell-sugar-water-for (archived at https://perma.cc/HL4D-3QWT)

Storefront [accessed 30 June 2019] The Seven Pillars of Pop-Up Shop Success [Online] www.thestorefront.com/mag/the-seven-pillars-of-pop-up-shop-success/ (archived at https://perma.cc/M7Z4-FNGE)

Think Forward Initiative [accessed 31 May 2019] Article #1: How an Accelerator and Research Challenges Are Bringing More Impact to Decision-Making [Online] www2.deloitte.com/nl/nl/pages/financial-services/articles/how-an-accelerator-and-research-challenges-are-bringing-more-impact-to-decision-making.html (archived at https://perma.cc/4L3H-KK7E)

Tuder, S [accessed 14 December 2017] Kellogg's Cafe Now Looms Over Union Square, Peddling Sugary Cereal For All [Online] https://ny.eater.com/2017/12/14/16777478/kelloggs-cafe-open-union-square (archived at https://perma.cc/UF5G-H9KN)

Chapter 5

Bernbach, W [accessed 30 June 2019] Bernbach's Quotes [Online] www.slideshare.net/nich_marketing/bernbach-quotes-9308977 (archived at https://perma.cc/L43N-UXRA)

British Business Bank [accessed 8 July 2019] Female Start-up Founders Missing out on Billions in Funding [Online] www.british-business-bank.co.uk/female-start-up-founders-missing-out-on-billions-in-funding/ (archived at https://perma.cc/3L3C-M7TR)

Collins, J (2001) *Good to Great*, Random House, London

Gladwell, M (2009) *What the Dog Saw and Other Adventures*, Little, Brown and Company, Boston, MA

Godin, S (2018) *This is Marketing: You can't be seen until you learn to see*, Penguin, Harmondsworth

Hall, R (2016) *Brilliant Marketing: How to plan and deliver marketing strategies – Regardless of the size of your budget*, 3rd edition, Pearson Business, London

Horowitz B (2014) *The Hard Thing About Hard Things: Building a business when there are no easy answers*, Harper Business, New York

Kahneman, D (2012) *Thinking, Fast and Slow*, Penguin, Harmondsworth

Maister, D H (2002) *The Trusted Advisor*, Simon & Schuster UK, London

Margin Call (2011) dir. J C Chandor

Mead, P (2014) *When in Doubt Be Nice: Lessons from a lifetime in business*, Silvertail Books, Kidderminster

Smart Business Trends [accessed 30 May 2019] Bill Gates' Quotes [Online] http:// smartbusinesstrends.com/tag/your-most-unhappy-customers-are-your-greatest-source-of-learning/ (archived at https://perma.cc/55W4-FXUT)

The Future Factory [accessed 8 July 2019] Agency Credentials and the Cobbler's Son [Online] https://thefuturefactory.co.uk/resources/get-your-agency-credentials-right/ (archived at https://perma.cc/6AX6-3E73)

Top Gun (1986) dir. A Scott

WeWork [accessed 30 May 2019] 2019 Global Impact Report [Online] https://impact.wework.com/ (archived at https://perma.cc/E6VN-P9EU)

Index